Crafting the Character Arc

A Practical Guide to Character Creation and Development

by Jennie Jarvis

Published 2014 by Beating Windward Press LLC

For contact information, please visit:
www.BeatingWindward.com

First Edition
ISBN: 978-1-940761-12-1

Table of Contents

Introduction

Many writers think that, just because they have their basic structure in place, their stories are destined to succeed. The problem with many narratives, however, can often come in those places between the plot points. Ensuring the story is moving forward in every scene often comes in the shape of a character arc. While many books on the craft of writing state that characters need to be three dimensional and change, a beginning writer isn't always sure how to turn these rather conceptual ideas into something a bit more concrete.

Based on her acclaimed workshop, author Jennie Jarvis has penned *Crafting The Arc*. This essential guide for writers takes the conceptual idea of the character arc and creates a step-by-step, practical guide for beginning writers to use in order to ensure they create characters both dynamic and engaging. Using narrative examples from multiple platforms, including novels, films, plays and games, this is the essential guide for helping writers create an active and well-defined character arc.

Crafting The Character Arc is structured in three main parts. Part One will consist of a more traditional approach to creating character, including personalities, depth, secrets, goals versus emotional needs, active versus reactive protagonists, and dramatic functions. All of these more traditional ideas about discussing character will set the reader up for the new information and approach they will be introduced to in Part Two.

Part Two will introduce the reader to the Major Dramatic Curve, a detailed pictorial representation of a character arc. The rest of this section will dedicate one chapter to each element of the Major Dramatic Curve, using the narrative examples introduced in Part One to provide detailed demonstrations of how each element works in a larger narrative.

Part Three will focus on practical applications of the Major Dramatic Curve and some variations in its use. First, the writer will be given step-by-step guidance on using the Curve to help him/her in the creation of their narrative work. Then, as any writer can attest, there are always exceptions to any rule, and this section will address several of those exceptions. Part Three will end with a call to action for the reader.

The appendix of this textbook provides reference information for the narrative examples used throughout the text to demonstrate the concepts discussed. These narrative examples will come from multiple platforms (novels, films, games, plays and web series) in order to show the versatility of the concepts discussed. Finally, a glossary is included for a quick and user friendly review of all the terms defined throughout this textbook.

This textbook will be intended for the beginning or intermediate writer aspiring to work in any narrative driven forms of storytelling. With its step-by-step guide to creating a character arc, it could serve as a useful textbook in any high school, community college, University or community/adult education program that teaches narrative creative writing, including traditional Creative Writing, Game Design, Playwriting programs or Film Schools.

This textbook will also serve as a unique and refreshing approach to the veteran writer looking for a new take on an old concept. Since the primary approach of creating a character arc in this book is based on the well-known paradigm of Freytag's triangle, it will also provide interest to any author who has studied this outdated concept and give them a new and modern approach to its use.

Part 1

Understanding Character

Whether a character in your novel is full of choler,
bile, phlegm, blood or plain old buffalo chips,
the fire of life is in there, too,
as long as that character lives.
— James Alexander Thom

Chapter 1
Why Another Book On Character?

If you are anything like me, you are most likely a bit annoyed at the large number of craft books on creating character. I have at least a dozen of them, sitting on my shelf gathering dust or burning up space in my eReaders. I read through each of them once and then never felt the need to go back to them again.

Whether you write novels, short stories, film screenplays, television or games, the character books all read the same way. They explore how you can build a personality by looking at the character's past. They ask you develop character bibles or bios, indicating the name of the uncle who molested them when they were seven or diagnosing their PTSD or ADHD or some other mental health ailment. They remind you to make sure your character is "fully developed" and "well rounded" and other vague terms that we understand but aren't completely sure how to execute in our own works.

Most of all, however, these books talk about how a character should "change" and "grow." Who they are at the end needs to be someone different than who they were at the beginning. This seems to make sense. After all, if a character hasn't changed, then why did we bother to go on a journey with them to begin with?

But… how do you get from point A to point B? How do you take the weakling child and turn her or him into the conquering hero? How do we take the character and pull them through their Arc?

This gap is where I get the most frustrated with my character craft books. I know where to begin, and I know where I want to end, but I don't always know the road in between. And those books do very little to help me along the way.

My frustration mostly comes from the fact that I was spoiled rotten when it came to learning plot development. My formal training came from screenwriting. Most non-film school students don't realize that writing for the movies is a very detailed and structured process. Screenwriters are given very defined guidelines for how their stories must be written. For years, the guidelines came from American screenwriting guru Syd Field. His book *Screenplay* (1979) pioneered the use of the "Three Act Structure" in American screenwriting. Basically just an updated version of the beginning-middle-end structure Aristotle discussed in *The Poetics*, Field's "Three Act Structure" breaks down the proportions of a film's plot into four sections.

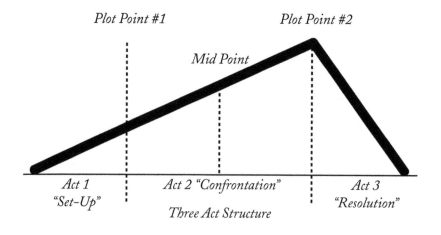

Plot Point #1   *Plot Point #2*

Mid Point

Act 1   *Act 2 "Confrontation"*   *Act 3*
"Set-Up"   *"Resolution"*

Three Act Structure

The first thirty pages of a screenplay were considered "Act One." Also known as "The Setup" or "Exposition", this section introduces the main characters and conflict of the story. Here, we meet the protagonist and see him/her begin his/her quest for the goal. This is also where we learn what the genre of the film will be. At the end of this Act, a major Plot Point (called "Plot Point One") occurs which heightens the stakes for the protagonist and really kicks off the main storyline.

The most famous Act One to Act Two change of all time can be seen in the classic film *The Wizard of Oz*. In Act One of the film, we meet Dorothy Gale, a bored teenager anxiously awaiting the start her life away from the farm on which she grew up. After a mean woman tries to put her precious dog Toto to sleep due to an off-screen incident of aggression, Dorothy and her dog run away from home. On the road, she meets a fortune teller who prophesizes her aunt is sick and might be dying. Dorothy turns around and runs home, but a powerful tornado hits the farm, transporting her and her dog to another world. Plot Point One is when Dorothy opens her front door and discovers she has arrived in a new world. This Act break is extremely famous because the film changes from black and white to vibrant color.

The next sixty pages of the script are called "Act Two," but it is divided into two smaller sections by the "Midpoint." The Midpoint is a major event that occurs exactly halfway through the story. This major event usually divides Act Two into two smaller quests that act as segments of the protagonist's main quest. For example, in *The Wizard of Oz*, Dorothy's overall goal is to get home to Kansas. In part one of Act Two, her quest is to go and see the Wizard. She meets him at the midpoint, and he tells her he will take her home only if she brings him the broomstick of the Wicked Witch of the West. This launches her into her second quest – to get the Witch's broom. She still wants to get home, but she has two different mini-quests that help her fight for her main goal. Since Act Two houses the majority of the main conflict of the story, Syd Field referred to this act as the "Conflict."

Act Two also ends with a Plot Point: "Plot Point Two." Plot Point Two is often referred to as the Point of No Return. Once the protagonist encounters this major plot point, she or he can never go back to the person she or he was at the beginning of the story. For Dorothy Gale, Plot Point Two is the moment she kills the Wicked Witch of the West. She is no longer the innocent girl she was at the beginning – running away and hiding. With the broomstick in her hand, she has grown from a child to a woman. She will never take her home for granted again, as she did in the opening of the film.

Syd Field called Act Three the "Resolution" of any screenplay, but this is often a very misleading term. While the third act contains the final scenes of the film, it's more than just the resolution. With an entire thirty pages of screenplay (or thirty minutes of film time), there has to be more than just "the ending" to fill up those pages. Often, this is the time when the protagonist must gather his or her resources and wits to overcome the main antagonist or villain. It's also where all subplots are resolved, and all themes are paid off. Good conquers evil. The girl gets the boy. And hey, is that a set-up for a sequel?

Looking at Act There of The Wizard of Oz, there is still quite a bit of plot left to finish the film. Dorothy and her friends return to the Emerald City, only to discover the Wizard is a fraud. While he can't magically transport her home, he agrees to take her in his hot air balloon. He gives gifts to each of Dorothy's friends, and then gets ready to take off. Toto runs off at the last moment, and Dorothy chases after him, the hot air balloon taking off without her. Finally, Glinda tells her she had the power all along to transport herself home. She clicks her heels together, and with a "there's no place like home", she returns to her aunt and uncle in the black and white world of Kansas, now a woman who appreciates what she has. The end.

This very strict 30-60-30 approach to screenplay writing evolved in 2005 when American screenwriter Blake Snyder released his own guide to screenplay structure entitled *Save the Cat: The Last Book On Screenwriting You'll Ever Need.* In this book, Snyder provided an extremely detailed page specific breakdown of how a plot should develop over time.

<u>Save The Cat "Beat Sheet"</u>
Opening Image (1)
Theme Stated (5)
Set-up (1-10)
Catalyst (12)
Debate (12-25)
Break Into Two (25)
B –Story (30)
Fun and Games (30-55)
Midpoint (55)
Bad Guys Close In (55-75)
All Is Lost (75)
Dark Night of the Soul (75-85)
Break Into Three (85)
Finale (85-110)

This "write by numbers" method became so popular in Hollywood, it was commonplace for a producer to open a screenplay to a specific page specifically to see if the screenwriter "knew what he was doing." While it was a great guidepost for beginning writers to learn structure, this constrictive formula is now criticized for making all major Hollywood films "feel" the same, regardless of genre.

I've never been a big fan of this overly constrictive plot structure in my writing, but I have to admit – when I was first learning how to write screenplays, I loved how the Three Act Structure gave me a very practical guide to follow when plotting out my story. Then, after I had been working in the film industry for a while, I marveled at how the *Save the Cat* Beat Sheet could help even the most aimless writer get back on track.

With such practical and definitive guidelines, I am frustrated by the very conceptual and intangible "let your character grow and change" I encountered in my craft books on creating character. It felt too conceptual and not practical enough to guide me through the development of my characters. I needed something more substantial to direct my writing.

In order to find a more hands on guide to creating character, I jumped into how narratives are studied in various formats. What I discovered was much more user-friendly and concrete than anything I experienced in the past, and I hope the information contained within this guide gives you the same clarity it gave me.

I've divided this book into three parts to help you create your own characters, whether you are writing novels, films, short stories, television shows, web series or even narrative-based video games. First, I explore the most basic ideas of character creation. We will define the term, exploring how a character can function within a text, and will look at some of those more conceptual approaches to character creation in case this happens to be your first character crafting book.

Next, I walk you through the practical guide I share with my students when it comes to character creation, namely The Major Dramatic Curve. As the Three Act Structure and the *Save the Cat* Beat Sheet provides screenwriters with step-by-step assistance in plot creation, the Major Dramatic Curve gives you step-by-step assistance in creating a fully developed Character Arc that will not only guide your characters through the narrative but will also allow for them to grow and change in a believable and identifiable process. Fortunately, however, where *Save the Cat* almost strangled the creativity out of some Hollywood films, the Major Dramatic Curve will act as a guide to enhance the character creation and development process instead of hindering it.

The final section of this text guides you, the writer, on your next step after reviewing this work. I give you instructions on how to practically apply the Major Dramatic Curve to your original creative works and address any variations to the Curve as it applies to non-traditional narrative structures.

Finally, the appendix is intended to be a practical and useful guide for you to use as you explore the pages of this textbook. I provide a short synopsis of a number of different narratives I use as examples. Even if you haven't read or seen these narratives, my hope is that the brief synopsis will give you enough information to make these examples useful to you. You may want to flip through these titles before you read this book so you are aware what we will be covering. If there is a narrative you have not yet read, seen or played, and you would like to explore it on your own before reading any plot points in this text (including potential spoilers), then I invite you to do that. I also provide you with a glossary you can use to look up any terms which might help you understand the materials discussed.

This text introduces some concepts and ideas you will initially feel a bit resistant to follow. After all, how can creativity be confined by such practical and specific guidelines? At the end of the day, your story is ultimately your story, and you will use whatever process works best for you. That being said, having taught the information and concepts in this text for over fifteen years, I have yet to encounter a single person who hasn't, in some way, benefited from studying the concepts detailed in this book. Even those who feel this process isn't for them have still taken away a new viewpoint that deepened their understanding of character as a whole.

Approach this text with an open mind and at least experiment with the suggestions in this book. Who knows? You may discover more about your characters than you ever thought possible.

Chapter 2
Understanding Character

Before we dive into the intricacies of building a character arc, it's important we take a step back and make sure we are on the same page when it comes to defining the word character. "Character" is one of those words whose definition becomes much more complex than the initial concept itself. It's like trying to define the word "creativity." Everyone thinks they know what it means, but if you asked a person to define it, he or she would stutter a bit. We all have a sense of what it is, but when you try to put it into words, you feel a bit lost. So let's walk through the process of defining character for our discussion in this book.

For writers, character is just a combination of traits, morals, personality and attitudes that make up the individuals who exist within our stories. These attributes are revealed by how the individual overcomes the barriers and surprises placed in his or her way. Character is a means to relate our plot to the reader or viewer, allowing them to experience the world of the story in a way that provides them with some kind of experience they wouldn't normally encounter in real life.

As writers, we see the worlds we create as our own, and we see our characters as belonging to us. This is *my* protagonist. That is *my* antagonist. We write out our fantasies and our nightmares, fulfilling our visions and wishes through our storytelling. But the sad truth is while we might create the world, it will ultimately belong to the readers who purchase our books or the viewers who watch the play, film or other form of entertainment developed from our scripts. We may start the creation process, but it is in their hands that our creations become complete.

Character is the reason people are willing to participate in the creation of our world. These readers/viewers want to find an escape from their lives, and identifying with the characters we create permits them to do this. By recognizing themselves in the individuals we write, it gives the reader/viewer a cathartic release, allowing them to feel the emotions they can't experience in their daily routine. When a viewer watches an action film, he sees himself as the hero, saving the day one explosion at a time. When a reader falls in love with the dashing yet socially awkward male main character, she sees herself being loved and cherished in return. A bored housewife can experience sexual bliss in a well written piece of erotica, and a stressed out college student can get rid of his own stress while seeing how a protagonist thwarts the murderous plans of a villain.

That's not to say all types of creative writing are intended to be escapist readings. Some writers choose to explore language with their stories; some just want to make money. Regardless of what the writer intended, the everyday reader or viewer wants to see themselves in the world they are witnessing through a novel, film or other narrative medium. Even if they are not reading for the sake of escapism, they still must be able to identify with the characters in order to go on the journey of the narrative.

Character is a gateway, opening the door between writer and experiencer. As writers, our job is to make sure each gateway we create is as unique, engaging, and believable as possible. While this means each personality needs to be different (and we will dive more into this in the next chapter), it also has much deeper implications. Not only does each character need to have a very unique temperament, but they need to have a purpose as well. These purposes are known as dramatic functions.

Dramatic Functions

When beginning to study or create character, one of the most important questions to ask is "What is the character's purpose?" The easiest answers to come up with are "the protagonist" or "antagonist," but dramatic functions can be much more complex than this. Almost every story out there contains more than just a protagonist and an antagonist, so we need to look at all those secondary characters and ask what they do and what purpose they serve. Harry Potter would be nothing without Ron and Hermione, but you can't call either of them the protagonist or the antagonist. So what are their purposes?

In order to evaluate the purpose of a character, it's important first to ask what that character's relationship is to the protagonist or antagonist. Often, beginning writers like to think of the protagonist as "the hero." This is true in many mainstream stories that utilize the classic trope of "good versus evil." Harry Potter is definitely a hero; he valiantly defeats Voldemort on multiple occasions. Dorothy is a hero as well. She defeats the Wicked Witch of the West. In *The Goonies*, Mikey escapes the murderous Fratellis and saves his neighborhood. In *The Dark Tower*, Roland saves the crumbling Tower, which in turns saves his world as well as our own. Link saves Zelda. Hamlet destroys the evil King Claudius. These are all heroes in the basic definition.

But what about those protagonists who aren't quite "heroes"? Elizabeth Bennett is definitely the protagonist of *Pride and Prejudice*, but can she be called a hero? She doesn't overcome evil. In her pride, she prejudges a good yet flawed man and treats him with contempt for the majority of the book. Doug in *The Town* is a bank robber and recovering drug addict who blows off his ex-girlfriend, throwing her aside in his attempt to lead a "clean" life. In *Wreck-It Ralph*, the protagonist is a popular video game villain who loses his temper and is so concerned about what other people think, he almost destroys the Candy Land video game world of *Sugar Rush*. While all of these characters are identifiable and heroic, they can't be called heroes without really stretching the definition of the word and forgiving them all their bad behaviors. So the word "hero" can't really be used when trying to define the protagonist.

A better definition for protagonist would be the single character whose primary goal drives the main storyline. Without this character, the rest of the story wouldn't exist. The character doesn't have to be the "lead" character (although he or she usually is), but it is the one character who makes the narrative wheel turn. Even in an ensemble or buddy movie, there is usually one protagonist who drives the story forward. In *Bill & Ted's Excellent Adventure*, Ted is the protagonist, not both of them. Ted is the one who has more to lose (he will be sent off to military school if they don't pass history). This makes him the driving force behind all of their actions, despite the buddy movie framing.

In *The Avengers*, Nick Fury is the protagonist, even though he has less screen time than most of the super heroes. After Loki steals the Tesseract, Fury assembles the main heroes in order to get it back and save the world. Even though Westley might be the "hero" of *The Princess Bride* because he rescues the damsel in distress, it is the Grandfather telling Westley's story to his Grandson that pushes the story forward, making him the protagonist (but more about him in Part Three). In the television show *Supernatural*, even though both brothers can be considered heroes (in season one, at least), the identity of the protagonist changes each week. Sometimes, Sam will be the protagonist of the episode because he is the primary force behind that week's show, but other times, Dean will be the one in charge. Does this make either of them less of a hero? No. They kill demons and monsters each week, so they are still the good force defeating bad, but they can't both be protagonists. Again, the protagonist is the driving force of the narrative – the character whose quest to achieve a goal is the entire reason why the story exists.

Conversely, the antagonist is the character whose goal most directly conflicts with the goal of the protagonist. Often, beginning writers will think this automatically makes the antagonist the villain, but this isn't always the case. The term "villain" implies evil, and an antagonist doesn't have to be evil. Think of romantic comedies. While there are sometimes "bad" characters, the antagonist is often the love interest. In *Pride and Prejudice*, Elizabeth Bennett tries to shame Darcy for insulting her when they first met, but he is trying to prove his worth to her. That makes him the antagonist, but not the villain. In *The Wizard of Oz*, Dorothy wants to go home. The Wizard refuses to help her unless she defeats the Wicked Witch. This makes the Wizard the antagonist, even if the Wicked Witch is the villain. In *Wreck-it Ralph*, Ralph wants to get his medal but Vanellope needs it to race. She might be annoying, but King Candy is the evil force in the story, not Vanellope. A "villain" can be an antagonistic force, but that doesn't always mean the villain is the antagonist. The antagonist's goal conflicts with the protagonist's goal, but this doesn't make her or him a bad person.

A wonderful film to explore when considering these major dramatic functions is the Disney animated film *Frozen*. The two main characters in the film, sisters Anna and Elsa, are both extremely flawed human beings who are products of a rather unhealthy upbringing. Due to her uncontrollable powers, Elsa has been told to oppress her feelings and hide from her emotions. Instead of helping, however, Elsa's fear has grown immensely, making her powers seem all the more unmanageable as a result.

Anna, on the other hand, has been sequestered away from any other child her age, and has grown a bit careless as a result. She's overly trusting and acts irrationally on multiple occasions, including accepting a marriage proposal from a man she just met. Neither of these characters can be called completely good or completely evil, so choosing a "hero" and a "villain" isn't as easy as it was in Disney movies of yesteryear (Aladdin = good, Jafar = bad, Belle = good, Gaston = bad, Rapunzel = good, Mother Gothel = bad, etc.).

Even if we ignore the question of good versus evil, it's still difficult to select a single protagonist for *Frozen*. Both sisters have wonderfully active and defined goals. Elsa wants to protect her sister from the power of her magic, and Anna wants her sister's friendship back. In the end, they both win their goal at almost the same moment. So how can you tell who is the "protagonist" and who is the "antagonist"? Remember, the protagonist is the character whose actions most directly drive the plot. In this film, the plot is a sister journeying into the snow in order to make amends and save her city. Therefore, Anna is the protagonist, and Elsa is the antagonist. This gives the title of "villain" to another, more minor character, the two-faced Prince Hans.

Now we have a sense of who the protagonist and the antagonist are, we can figure out what the dramatic functions of the secondary characters. No character in a narrative should be there because the writer needed them to say a line or to fill in the background. All characters should have a solid and definable purpose for being in the story.

Since it's such a great ensemble piece, let's look at *Harry Potter and the Sorcerer's Stone* (or *Philosopher's Stone* for non-US readers). We have established that Harry Potter is both protagonist and hero, but what about the other characters? Here's a simple breakdown of several of the supporting characters of that first book.

Character: Ron Weasley
Dramatic Function: Ally, Emotional Support, Serves as a double for Harry since he is another "outsider" in the world of wizards, As Harry's best friend, he also serves as a "confessional" character, allowing Harry to express himself to the readers via Ron

Character: Hermione Granger
Dramatic Function: Ally, Provides exposition and other important information the reader needs to know, If there is anything the reader needs to know, Hermione fills us in as she explains it to Harry.

Character: Albus Dumbledore
Dramatic Function: Another expositional character able to reveal the secrets that a mere student like Hermione would not logically know, serves as Mentor and a source for the most advanced magic (basically, JK Rowling says "I want this to happen, so Dumbledore can make it so and the reader will believe it"), he also tends to be the character who can analyze the story and express the theme to the reader.

Character: Neville Longbottom
Dramatic Function: Comic relief, serves as another "double" for Harry, he also shows that Harry is not the worst person there. Since the reader identifies with Harry, we don't want to feel like the loser of the class, and so we are able to laugh at Neville's misfortunes in order to feel better about our own point of identification

Character: Peeves the Poltergeist
Dramatic Function: Another source of comic relief, serves as a world building tool to help set up the rules of the afterlife in this world, in a few select chapters, he is the justification for why certain things happen (Harry, Ron, Hermione and Neville

running from Filch because Peeves alerted him, for example), he also served as the red herring in the first book as many students believed he let in the troll and not Quirrell.

Character: Severus Snape
Dramatic Function: The major red herring and false villain in this book, because of his obvious dislike for Harry and his appearance, he is assumed to be the evil force chasing the philosopher's/sorcerer's stone.

Character: Draco Malfoy
Dramatic Function: Antagonist (Harry's role involves finding validation in this new wizarding world, and Malfoy's goal of destroying him most directly conflicts with that goal), he also serves as a foil to Harry and a model example of the "typical" Slytherin student.

Character: Quirinus Quirrell
Dramatic Function: As an extension of Voldemort, this is the true villain of the narrative. He is the driving force behind all the dastardly deeds going on at Hogwarts. His goal of finding the philosopher's stone drives the main mystery of the story and provides multiple obstacles to Harry's goal of blending in and being accepted by the wizarding world.

There are many more characters in the book, but the above examples should be enough to show you that each character has a very specific purpose in the plot. None of them are just walking around talking because JK Rowling thought they were funny or wanted to give a friend a cameo. They all have a dramatic function.

Let's Go Back To The Bloke That Really Matters

Now that we understand how characters function in a text, let's go back to the protagonist for a bit. As stated above, the protagonist is the character whose primary goal drives the main storyline. But what if you are working with a protagonist whose goal isn't well-defined? What if your story features a character who is more reactive than active?

The argument on whether or not this is acceptable is still out for debate. For every author or analyst who claims you *must* have an active protagonist, there are at least two examples of successful stories where the protagonist is reactive. The popular "Hero's Journey" structure even includes a section of the journey where the protagonist is supposed to "deny the call", passively resisting the goal instead of fighting to win it. The Hero's Journey is one of the most popular structures of epic storytelling, so is it "wrong" to ask a protagonist to be reactive, if only for a short period? Again, the jury is out, but I argue that it's always best to aim for an active protagonist.

Twilight is a great example of why I think an active protagonist is best. Whether you like the series or not, both the movies and the books demonstrate the positive and the negative sides to having a reactive or active protagonist. In many ways, this reactive versus active issue might actually explain why you are or are not a fan.

In the first book in the series, Bella doesn't really have an active goal. She is reacting to Edward more than fighting to win any kind of goal (unless you want to argue her goal is to "understand" him, which isn't an active verb and therefore, not an active goal). This is a very successful narrative financially, especially after its adaptation into a successful box office film series, but it also polarized audiences. At the height of its success, people either loved it or hated it. It was rare to find anyone who rested somewhere in between when the films first hit theaters.

Audiences who loved it fell for the dramatic elements of the film, emotionally identifying with Bella's position as a rather lackluster protagonist who attracts the attention of a mysterious and gorgeous stranger. Audiences who hated it despised that same drama, thinking it was creepy for a hundred-year-old man to become fascinated by a young and rather boring high school girl. So who was right?

The answer lies in the second book, *New Moon*. While some audiences still shunned the second book and film because of their dislike for *Twilight*, there was an overall stronger reception to this second story than the first. The characters and world were the same, so what changed? One simple thing: Bella became an active protagonist, taking charge of her fate instead of just sitting around and letting Edward stare at her. In *Twilight*, Bella spent most of the book reacting to Edward's mysterious ways instead of trying to pursue him. In *New Moon*, however, Bella has an active goal. Edward has left her, and she wants him back. She is willing to do anything to get him. When she discovers an ability to see his face any time she comes close to death, she commits a series of death-defying stunts to summon him. This included everything from riding a motorcycle too fast to jumping off a mountain. Now *that's* being an active protagonist.

As mentioned before, readers and viewers want to experience a vicarious adventure when they disappear into the worlds we create. If the character we identify with doesn't actively pursue a goal, then what do we, as readers or viewers, gain as a result of experiencing their journey with them? I'm not saying that Bella's actions in the first book were "wrong," but I want the readers of my books and the viewers of my films to gain something from their time with my narrative. Therefore, I believe if authors want to be successful, it's best to focus on active goals.

Goals Versus Needs

Many beginning writers confuse a goal with a need, and it's easy to understand why. There are other character books out there that examine these two concepts much deeper than I will here, so if you still find yourself confused after reading this section, I recommend you spend more time exploring these two terms.

A goal (sometimes called a character's "want") is something a character fights for that has a very obvious outcome. You should always be able to point a camera at the outcome of a goal, even if you aren't writing a film. In *Wreck It Ralph*, Ralph wants a medal that will prove he's a hero. In *The Dark Tower*, Roland wants to keep the Tower from crumbling. In *Wizard of Oz*, Dorothy wants to get home. In *The Legend of Zelda*, Link wants to save Zelda. In *Dr. Horrible's Sing-Along Blog*, Dr. Horrible wants to be admitted to the Evil League of Evil. In *Gone Girl*, Nick wants to get his wife back. These are all visual goals for which you could take a picture of the outcome. They are tangible and real.

Most importantly, however, there is no question whether or not the protagonist has won or lost their goal at the end. When your reader or viewer comes to the end of your story, they should know that the character's journey is officially over. If a character just wants to "be happy," then how will the reader know if he or she has won that goal? We can all be happy for a moment, but unhappy the next. So we want to ask ourselves what does it mean for this particular character to be happy? Will it be the moment they get married? Or win the Quidditch Cup? Or kill the villain? Picking these more concrete goals makes it really clear when the character's story is over.

Many writers like to use a Major Dramatic Question to help them figure out whether or not they have picked a strong goal. A Major Dramatic Question is literally a question that should be answered with a yes or no by the end of the story. It is structured liked this:

Will __(protagonist)__ __(active verb)__ __(object)__ ?

For example, the Major Dramatic Question for *The Wizard of Oz* is "Will __Dorothy__ __return__ __home__?"

We know this is a solid goal because we can answer this question with a YES, and we can name the specific moment where it happens (she wakes up and sees her Aunt and Uncle standing above her – this is important because she wants to return both to the physical location of home as well as the more conceptual idea of home, which is embodied by her family). Throughout the story, Dorothy is constantly and actively fighting to answer that question with a yes. As soon as she succeeds, her story is over and the book or film can end.

Another, slightly more advanced example comes from *Hamlet*: Will Hamlet avenge his father's death? Many first-time Hamlet readers might make the mistake of thinking Hamlet's goal is to kill Claudius. While that eventually becomes the tactic that Hamlet uses to win his goal, it was not his overall goal. The ghost who approaches Hamlet at the beginning of the play claims to be Hamlet's father, but Hamlet isn't going to kill his own uncle without proof that the ghost was actually his father and not some vengeful demon pretending to be his father. So, first, he verifies that his father's soul actually needs vengeance before taking the next step. Once he has verified that his uncle killed his father, he moves in to kill him, but finds Claudius praying. Hamlet believed that killing his uncle while he prayed would actually send him to Heaven, and that wouldn't be the vengeance he wanted. So Hamlet waited to catch Claudius doing something that would send his soul to Hell before killing him. Once Claudius accidentally murdered his own wife with the poisoned wine, Hamlet was free and clear to kill the king, thereby answering his Major Dramatic Question with a resounding yes!

Asking the Major Dramatic Question is a great tool for writers who feel their characters often become unfocused on their goal. The writer can ask if the character is actively fighting to answer that question with a yes in every scene. If, at any time, the character has forgotten to answer that question, then the writer knows he or she needs to go back and refocus. Just like there should be only one goal for the main character, there should be only one Major Dramatic Question as well.

While a character can only have one goal and one Major Dramatic Question for a story, there can be many needs. A need is something more emotional or conceptual. The character would like to have this need fulfilled, and the narrative gives them a chance to gain that need by winning their goal. In other words, fulfilling the need will be a byproduct of winning the goal. In many instances, it is the needs of the character - not the goal - the reader or viewer remembers the character pursuing.

The needs are often the emotional motivators for the protagonist to win his or her goal. In *Wreck It Ralph*, winning a medal will allow Ralph to feel accepted. In *The Goonies*, finding the treasure will allow Mikey to keep the community he loves (both in terms of property and on a more conceptual basis). In *Gone Girl*, getting his wife back will allow Nick to prove he is the "good guy," appeasing his fear of turning out like his jerk-father. In *Pride and Prejudice*, Elizabeth needs to feel validated after Darcy's insult. Harry Potter needs to feel like he belongs since he spent his entire childhood being told he is worthless. These needs are all different than the more visual goals the characters are fighting for, but they are equally important to the story.

A great example to look at more closely is *Dr. Horrible's Sing-Along Blog*. His goal is to be inducted into the Evil League of Evil. He wins this goal when we see him walk into the Evil League of Evil Boardroom, all suited up in his fancy red suit. Why does he want to win this goal? What are his emotional motivators? For one, he *needs* to prove that he is worthy of the girl of his dreams, Penny. He is too shy to speak to her in real life, and he thinks that getting into the League is the only way to prove his worth. He also *needs* to fix the world around him. He thinks it is corrupt and faulty. Getting into the League is the only way he can be in a position of power that will allow him to make changes. Finally, he *needs* to validate his own existence. Captain Hammer has been treating him like an insignificant nothing for so long, he doesn't have faith in himself. Getting into the League would prove his worth as a human being. It would allow him to fulfill his need for revenge against his "super hero" bully.

The needs are the motivations that drive him to win his goal, and his goal is what drives the primary story of this narrative. When a writer takes the time to build a character from scratch, these are the layers that need to be considered before a single word of the actual narrative is attempted. In the puzzle of character creation and development, all the pieces fit together into a seamless and well-crafted whole.

Crafting Your Character

It's time to start thinking about the character whose story you want to write. In order to prepare, consider the following:

1. Who is your protagonist? How does that person's story drive the narrative forward? Is your protagonist active or reactive? If you chose to make your protagonist reactive, how can you take that same character and make her or him active?

2. How will your reader/viewer identify with this protagonist? In what way will your readers/viewers see themselves in this main character?

3. What is your protagonist's Goal? How will the audience know, for a fact, whether this character has won or lost?

4. What are the emotional motivators (needs) driving your protagonist towards winning her or his goal? These should NOT be the same as the goal.

5. Think of your supporting characters. List out each character, their dramatic function, goal and needs. Which character has the strongest antagonistic impact on your protagonist? Remember, the antagonist doesn't have to be the villain.

6. What is the Major Dramatic Question for your protagonist? Does it follow the "Will (protagonist) (active verb) (object)" structure? If not, can you find a way to make it fit? Remember, you should be able to answer this question with a very clear YES or NO. A YES tells us the protagonist won the goal. A NO tells us the protagonist lost the goal.

7. Why do you want to write this character's story? How is this character a reflection of you or your psyche? If you can't see yourself in your character, then why are you writing it? What can you bring to this story that no other writer could?

Chapter 3
The Personality of Character

I would be remiss to write a book on character where I didn't allow you to dive into the all too familiar world of character building by developing the personality of a character. This is, after all, what most of us think of when it comes to Character creation. What does my character look like? Is she sarcastic? Is he intelligent? What's his astrological sign? What happened to them when they were three and left at the mall by their mother? All of these character questions are well trodden and familiar, but they are still important to note.

When it comes to building a character's personality, there are two major things worth considering: The character's persona and the mechanics of how the personality is conveyed to the reader.

Character Persona

Building a character's persona is a lot like playing with Legos. You have a large variety of pieces that can be put together in different ways to create all kinds of unique and interesting combinations. Even though we all have the same building blocks (hair colors, occupations, religions, etc.), my character will come out much differently than yours. In *The Lego Movie*, while trying to escape Cloud Cuckoo Land, the team of Lego heros all tried to build a submarine. Each character's portion of the sub was unique, reflecting their unique personalities. Unikitty built a rainbow section. Batman only works in black ("and sometimes very, very dark gray"). Benny used retro spaceship pieces. And Emmet... he built his double decker couch.

Let's take a look at some of the character pieces we have to work with:

Physical Attributes: Hair color, eye color, height, build, etc.

Special Physical Features: Scars, different color eyes, unique birthmarks, limps, tattoos

Ethnicity: This applies to both racial ethnicity and cultural ethnicity. You can mix and match as needed.

Occupation: What do they do for a living? Are they happy with this job?

Social Status: It's important to look at this not only in terms of how much money they make but also in terms of how well they fit in with their peers. They might be rich but fit in better with a middle class or low class income family.

Family: Are they married or single? Do they stay in contact with their parents? Are their parents divorced? Do they have any siblings? What about children? And how do they feel about family as a whole?

Sexuality: Don't just look at the very general ideas of straight or gay, but look at all the shades in between as well (i.e. bisexual, transgender, straight but has considered bisexuality, straight but has non-traditional sexual habits, etc.). You can also look at what kind of lover they are: tender, aggressive, dominant, submissive, kinky, vanilla, etc.

Intelligence: Remember to think about book smarts, street smarts and emotional intelligence as well as skill mastery (good with computers, bad with car mechanics, etc.).

Relationship with others: How does the character get along with other people? How does their way of dealing with other people change based on the kind of people? Are they selfless or selfish?

Relationship with self: What does the character think about him or herself? Do they do kind things for themselves (eat right, get massages, etc.) or do they treat themselves poorly (starve or overeat, spend more time helping others than themselves, etc.)?

Relationship with subordinates: A lot can be shown about a character's true personality when we see how they treat a waiter, customer service representative or telemarketer. How well do they tip? Do they answer a telemarketing call with patience or anger? We can also learn a lot from how they treat animals. Do they have any pets?

Educational experience: Look both in terms of how much schooling they completed and how they view themselves as a result (i.e. proud of their three graduate degrees or believing they need more to prove they are smart).

Psychology: Don't jump to label someone with ADHD, PTSD or OCD if you haven't done your research or fully understand the mental disorder. But keep in mind that sibling rivalry, poor self-image, a desire to not turn out like their parent and other more nuanced mental views can be worth exploring as well.

Religion and morality: These could very easily be divided into two categories since a religious person does not always have morals and vice versa. However, I have paired them together because it is important to question how a character's relationship with God (or lack thereof) affects her or his moral stance.

Astrological Impact: Picking the character's birthday and matching sign can help you pick his/her primary personality traits. Looking at their rising or moon signs can add another layer of depth as well.

Safe spaces: Where does the character feel the most comfortable? In her or his messy one room flat or in the chic and clean office? Does the character only feel comfortable on a subway train?

Fashion: Look not only at how the character dresses (name brand versus thrift shopper) but also on how the character's appearance effects the way others look at him or her.

Eating habits: Healthy food or fast food? What's the character's favorite restaurant?

Relationship to Authority: Does the character do what he or she is told? Does he buck the system? Does she swear off all chain restaurants in order to "stick it to the man"?

Point of view: How does the character see the world? Are her glasses rose colored or deeply tinted?

Fears and Superstitions: What are both the logical and illogical fears of your character? Does she believe she will get seven years bad luck if she breaks a mirror? Is he afraid of the tree outside his window?

Culture: How does the character enjoy the world around him or her - through books, theater, music, movies, eating? What kinds of music does the character enjoy (even rage metal is a form of culture)?

Chronic conditions: Has the character suffered from a lifelong illness? Or maybe an obsession with an unworthy lover?

Character actions: Does the character always do what she says she will do? Does he say one thing and then do another? Does she act like she is mean but then save a cat from a tree? Does he say nothing but then save an empire?

Secret Item in the Closet: What tangible item do they keep hidden in their closet from even their closest friends?

I left the Secret Item In the Closet last on the list above because it is worth spending a bit more time exploring. Anytime we build a character, it's always good to give them a secret. In *The Goonies*, Mikey doesn't really need his inhaler. In *Pride and Prejudice*, Elizabeth hides her growing love for Darcy from everyone except her sister. Harry Potter never tells Ron and Hermione that the Sorting Hat wanted to put him in Slytherin. Obi-Wan took the secret of Luke's father's identity (Darth Vader) to his grave.

Each of these characters keeps or reveals their secrets for various reasons, but all of the secrets wind up giving the character additional depth. Let's look at Harry Potter's secret about almost getting sorted into Slytherin. Since many "bad" wizards come from Slytherin, Harry fears he might have some "bad" lurking inside of him and that is why he was almost placed in the "house that bad built." This is seen most clearly in *Chamber of Secrets* when Harry begins to question whether or not he might be the heir of Slytherin. He knows he has traits similar to Voldemort, including an orphan upbringing, a thirst to prove himself and the ability to speak Parseltongue. When students wind up petrified around the school, his worst fears begin to come true. People start to think he is the cause of all the attacks, and he is ostracized as a result. Holding onto the secret of his almost-sorting burns a hole inside his chest until he finally reveals the secret to Dumbledore, who kindly explains to him why he is able to speak Parseltongue. That burning secret allowed Rowling to play with Harry's internal struggle, adding to the overall conflict of the story and drawing in readers.

Having a secret also gives the writer a chance to play with subtext. A character might say one thing but we know he or she means something else because of that secret. As humans, we rarely say exactly what we mean, and it is often because of a secret. Here's an example: A friend asks us to read their short story. We think it is terribly written (secret), but we don't want to hurt them (justification for keeping that secret). Therefore, what we say to our friend isn't completely the truth. We want to help them but not hurt them, so we "soften" the truth. If we gave this interaction to a character, then the character's true feelings about the short story is the subtext.

The Secret Item in the Closet is a great tool for the writer to play with in order to help him or her discover their character's secret. For example, if a high school football player secretly hides university acceptance letters in his closet, we get to ask why. Is it because he doesn't want people to know he is brainy or yearns to go to school for an "unmanly" or other non-football degree? What are the implications of hiding that secret? What will happen when the deadline to accept the admission passes? Another example could be seen if a woman hides a photo of a man in her closet. Who is this man? Is it a long lost love? Or perhaps a twin brother whose death hangs on her conscious? What are the implications of that photo being found? Will her husband think she is cheating? Will her parents, determined to forget about their lost son, shun her? Having an emotional secret is wonderful for character building, but making that secret tangible allows for many more consequences and plot development.

All of the categories to consider regarding Character Persona are well worth exploring in terms of both character development and plot development since a well-developed plot should always be a side effect of well-written characters. I've seen some writers assign just one or two words to each category on the chart, but I often find writing a *minimum* of two to three paragraphs on each section tends to be the most advantageous when exploring a character's personality. Often, as we write, our pen or computer screen will miraculously begin unveiling to us more and more about our character. In the world of character building, it is always a good idea to do more character building than we need to do. The characters should be fully developed, even if the writer doesn't reveal all the information to the reader or viewer. You don't HAVE to use all the details you come up with, but it is great for YOU to know.

The Mechanics of Personality: Dialogue

I'm always amazed at how often the down and dirty mechanics of character dialogue are ignored. By mechanics, I mean the technical tools used by writers via dialogue. In other words, how the character's unique word choices and grammar reflect who they are as an individual.

When writing dialogue, I've attended workshops and read books where authors discuss how it's important to know whether a character has an accent or not, but I don't see much more than that. Ironically, it was in my years studying acting when I learned the most about dialogue mechanics. As part of my formal education, we were taught how to break down dialogue as a means for discovering character. By reverse engineering this analysis, I use character to help me determine my dialogue mechanics.

We've all heard that each character needs to have a unique and compelling voice, but what are the individual mechanical tools we can use to create those voices? Here are a few to consider while building your character's dialogue:

Diction (Word Choice): Does the character use big words or small words? Were they educated and can use "$5" words or is their experience with language limited? Do they swear? Do they use made up words or overly poetic words/phrases?

Length of sentences: When the character speaks, does she use fragment sentences or complete sentences? Does he use run on or compound sentences? Do they use a lot of extra, unneeded words or do they try to be as succinct as possible?

Length of speeches: This is an extension of length of sentences. When a character's line of dialogue goes on for an extended (more than three sentences) period of time, just how long does it go on for? Do they like to monologue? While this can vary a bit throughout the text, how long a character speaks will reflect how they see themselves.

Sentence Structure (Syntax): While most native English speakers are taught to use the traditional subject-verb-object sentence construction, this is not universal across the world.

Is their native language different than the one they currently speak? If so, then the way they structure their sentences may not be quite as linear. The most famous example of a character whose dialogue reflected a creative use of syntax is Yoda. ("Judge me by my size, do you?" – verb, object, subject).

Imagery: What kind of imagery does the character use? Does he have a poetic soul and tend to relate everything to some romantic or dramatic context? Is she a cynic whose metaphors and similes tie everything she sees with death or destruction? Or perhaps the character has no imagination or works in a very structured field, like computer programming or accounting, and therefore uses no imagery at all.

Delivery: How does a character speak the messages inside her head? Is she eloquent and can say exactly what she wants to say at all times? Or does her delivery depend on who she speaks to? Perhaps when she speaks to her boss, she uses complete sentences and confident imagery, but the moment her lifelong crush shows up, she stutters, uses no imagery and constantly uses words incorrectly.

Accent: While I mentioned this before, it's worth mentioning again – Does the character have an accent? I've met so many American writers who automatically default to using American standard – not because they aren't creative but because they just didn't think about doing something else. We live in a multicultural world, and how language works is changing based on that international influence.

Another item I encourage my students (especially my screenwriters) to think about when it comes to character dialogue is catch phrases. If you were going to place your character's face on a t-shirt and include one line of their dialogue that reflects their character, what would it be? This line can be said by the character him/herself or it can be said by another character. Either way, that one-liner helps define the personality of the character.

I love looking at the 2012 film *The Avengers* for this since, as an action film, it is packed full of them. Here are a few catch phrases that can easily define our favorite super hero characters:

Iron Man:
   "Genius, billionaire, playboy, philanthropist"
   "Maybe we can't protect the earth, but you can be damn sure we'll avenge it."
   ...Pretty much every line he says

Captain America:
   "It seems to be powered by some sort of electricity."
   "Call it Cap"

The Hulk:
   "Puny God"
   "Hulk… smash."
   "Well then son… You've got a condition"

Black Widow:
   "Regimes fall every day. I tend not to weep over that, I'm Russian."
   "I've been compromised."

With each character, these small, quotable lines give us a sense of who they are or how they see the world, regardless of whether they said the line or someone else said it to/about them.

From all the Avengers characters, my favorite dialogue comes from Loki. The ostracized younger son who grew tired of living in his older brother's shadow, Loki's dialogue reflects his character in a unique way and reflected not only who he was but how his position changed throughout the film:

Diction: Loki sees himself as a poetic hero in many ways, and you can see this in his choice of words. He loves to use the words that flow from the tongue: dripping, virtuous, tortured. Growing up in a royal family, he received a strong education, and this poetic choice of words reflects this. It is interesting to note, however, that you will almost never catch Loki using curse words regardless of how evil he might think himself. We can imagine that he sees those "vulgar" words as beneath him.

Length of Sentences: Once again, Loki's dialogue is more like poetry than anything. As such, his sentences are always flowery but never too long. When he gets really ramped up, he will use a few compound sentences, but for the most part, he uses short sentences that sound like they are longer than they are due to their poetic nature.

Length of Speeches: Loki is a monologuer, and this is used to great effect throughout the film. He feels the most power when he can speak for long periods of time. From his first appearance in the film, Loki neutralizes the SHIELD agents and then begins his "glad tidings" monologue in which he explains his theory that freedom is a lie. In each scene where Loki appears, the audience can expect a monologue or at least an attempt at a monologue.

Sentence Structure/Syntax: Loki's syntax reflects both his alien heritage and his poetic speaking style. He often strays from the strict subject-verb-object structure in order to deliver his lines with a bit more polish. He also loves to ask questions – most of them rhetorical – as part of his poetical style. i.e. "What have I to fear?"

Imagery: Loki loves his poetic imagery, but what's fascinating is how he changes from peaceful images to more violent ones when he tries to be threatening. When he is calm, he frames the idea of taking away people's freedom as a form of "peace," but when he gets angry, his imagery turns violent, focusing on "blood" and "ruin."

Delivery: One of my favorite things about Loki is how his dialogue patterns change throughout the film. Whenever he needed to be the punchline of a joke, Whedon would contrast his usually long, verbose speech patterns with a shorter or even a fragment sentence (i.e. "I'm listening" and "If it's all the same to you, I'll have that drink now."). Even better, however, is how his speeches grow progressively shorter as he loses power. At the beginning of the film, he delivers his long speeches without interruption, but as the Avengers grow together as a team, his speeches get cut down shorter and shorter (i.e. when Coulson shoots him or when the Hulk thrashes him like a rag doll).

Accent: Loki's accent is a throwback to what we would assume an ancient, civilized culture would sound like. It's two parts upper class British and one part poetry. Thor's accent is very similar, although his delivery is a bit rougher.

Catch phrases: "An ant has no quarrel with a boot." "I am burdened with glorious purpose." "It is the unspoken truth of humanity that you crave subjugation." "Freedom is life's great lie. Once you accept that, you will know peace."

By just looking at Loki's dialogue, we get a strong sense of his character. This wasn't done on accident. Writer/Director Joss Whedon knew how to manipulate the dialogue in order to reflect Loki's character. This made Loki a three-dimensional character that we really loved to hate.

When it comes time to really build the personality of your character, there are many ways to do this. Some people like to develop character bibles while others love to create vision boards. I've seen writers keep entire journals dedicated to one character, and I've seen Pinterest boards used to fully realize a persona. Regardless of which method works for you, it's important to take the time to understand your character's goals, needs, personality and dialogue mechanics before moving into writing your character's story.

It's also extremely important to understand how the personality of your character determines the methods he or she will use in order to win their goal. We will get into that in much more detail throughout the rest of this book.

Part 2

The Major Dramatic Curve

Plot is people.
Human emotions and desires
founded on the realities of life,
working at cross purposes,
getting hotter and fiercer
as they strike against each other
until finally there's an explosion
—that's Plot.
— Leigh Brackett

Chapter 4
The Major Dramatic Curve?

So now that we have a firm grasp of what a character is, how to shape a character's personality and, most important, how to identify the character's goal, it's time to get onto the good stuff: how to craft everything that you have created into an effective Character Arc.

At its most simplistic level, a Character Arc is the process of development a character goes through over the course of a narrative. He or she starts out the story as one person and then, as a result of going through a number of obstacles, trials, disappointments, and turmoil, he or she changes/morphs/evolves into another. In *Pride and Prejudice*, Elizabeth Bennett changes from being full of pride and filled with outlandish delight, not caring what anyone else thinks of her, to being slightly humbled and open minded, ashamed of her past arrogance. In *The Goonies*, Mikey starts off the film as weak and asthmatic, wanting to follow the rules and scolding his friends for not adhering to his parents' restrictions. By the end of the film, he has stopped believing the adults have all the answers or that the younger kids need to rely on someone other than themselves to achieve their dreams. He throws away his inhaler and becomes a leader in his gang. The character's change is responsible for our engagement in these stories. It's what we pay for when we buy the book or movie ticket.

But there are stories where the protagonist doesn't really change his personality as a result of his journey. Part of the chilling impact of the movie *There Will Be Blood* is seeing Daniel Plainview tackle anything in his way in order to accomplish his goal but not changing as a result. He goes through everything from getting baptized to committing murder and disowning his son, but none of these events has an effect on his emotions. It is this lack of change that makes for a terrifying portrayal of the man. Does that make his story have any less of a character arc?

To answer this question, let's look to the world of games. These playable narratives, especially older ones, rarely show a change in the protagonist, but they still connect with players in a way that other stories might not. *The Legend of Zelda* is one of Nintendo's most popular game series of all times. From the very earliest versions of the game, players loved to get into the shoes of Link as he fought his way through Hyrule in his attempt to rescue the Princess Zelda from Ganon. Link's personality doesn't change – partially because of what the technology was capable of when the series first began, but also because he didn't need to change. He had a strong and playable goal, and we cheered with him as he overcame each obstacle and moved closer to his goal. When he won his goal (saved Zelda), we also won– not only because we were the player who pushed the buttons to make it happen, but also because we were so engaged in his story that we experienced the cathartic release only narratives can provide.

As long as a character's goal develops over time (in other words, the tactics and obstacles evolve over the course of the story), then Character Arc doesn't have to be defined by personality change. In this case, the key to having a solid character arc is to make sure the entire struggle of the character's attempt to win his or her goal is covered within the narrative, in its entirety, in a unique and compelling way. Keep in mind, though, when I say we need to see his or her "entire" struggle, this doesn't mean we need to see every event from the moment the character was born to the moment the character dies. We just need the meat of the story, and that doesn't necessarily include a personality change (although the authors of many successful stories have chosen to show some kind of personality change).

As we discussed in Chapter Two, the primary function of a protagonist is to allow the reader or viewer to become a part of the world into which they are being introduced. This means the character's story needs to be set up in such a way that allows a door to open for them, permitting them to step out of their mundane world into a life of intrigue and drama (or comedy, action, fantasy, insanity, etc.). They need to step into the world at a period in the character's development where they can relate to what's happening. Then, they need to see how the character's life changes forever, dragging them along the adventure. They need to ride the roller coaster of emotion as the protagonist attempts to win his or her goal, and then celebrate with them when they win or mourn with them when they lose. If the readers/viewers aren't present for all of these steps, they can't experience the catharsis that motivated them to participate in the story to begin with.

So how can we, as writers, provide this kind of experience for our readers or viewers? How can we make sure the character's struggle and change are successfully integrated into our stories, regardless of whether we are writing a flash fiction piece, novel, film, game, play, web series or anything else under the sun? The answer is simple: we use the Major Dramatic Curve.

The Major Dramatic Curve

The Major Dramatic Curve is based on the work of 19th century German theater analyst Gustav Freytag. He wrote a study on the five-act structure used by many playwrights penning the theatrical productions of his day. In this study, he labeled each of the five acts with a different dramatic function (that is, their underlying purpose for existing within the play): exposition, rising action, climax, falling action and revelation/catastrophe (depending on if the play was a comedy or a tragedy).

Freytag's breakdown of dramatic functions was pictorially represented in a triangular shape meant to visualize the overall arc of the story. This pictorial representation came to be known as Freytag's triangle.

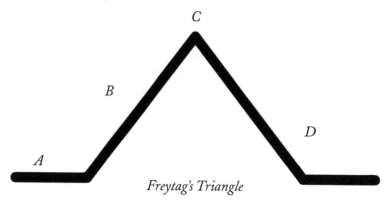

Freytag's Triangle

A) Exposition
B) Introduction of Conflict and Rising Action
C) Climax
D) Falling Action and Resolution.

Theater is a character driven medium, and so Freytag's analysis of how to break down the various acts of a play naturally transitioned over time into an analysis of how to break down character in any narrative genre. Similarly, the triangle morphed into a pictorial representation of a character's arc. This new triangle is what we know today as The Major Dramatic Curve.

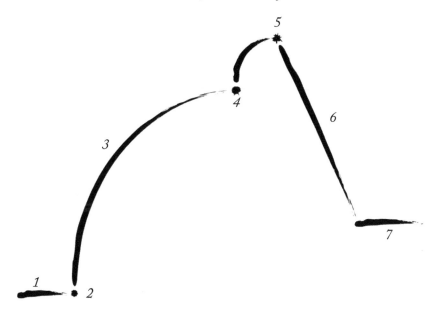

The Major Dramatic Curve has seven important elements. Each element occurs on a very specific and fixed point on the Curve. Each of these elements relate directly to a period in the development of the character:

1) The Resting Period
2) The Inciting Incident
3) The Rising Action
4) The Crisis Point
5) The Climax
6) The Falling Action
7) The New Resting Period (also known as the Resolution)

It is important when writing a narrative (film, especially, but this is also true for theater, television, comics, games, web series, short stories and novels) for the writer to include *all* of the basic components of the Major Dramatic Curve in his/her portrayal of their protagonist. The readers or viewers participate in a narrative because they want some form of cathartic release, and they can't get it if they don't go on this entire journey with the protagonist.

It is also nice when the entire Curve is presented for the antagonist, but this is not essential. Since the antagonist is the primary force keeping the protagonist from winning his or her goal, we become just as invested in their characters as we do the protagonist. In *Harry Potter and the Sorcerer's/Philosopher's Stone*, we get to see Voldemort's entire journey, even if some of it is revealed in backstory. We know who he was before his fall. We know his overall goal is to defeat Harry Potter. We know he began fighting for this goal the moment his killing curse rebounded, destroying himself instead of "the boy who lived." Over the course of the series, we also get to see Voldemort regaining strength, experiencing moments of doubt and, ultimately, his downfall. The entire Curve is present for him, even though he isn't the protagonist. This gives him as much literary power in the series as Harry Potter himself, even though The Dark Lord isn't present in every book. Seeing his entire Curve gives him a power that subconsciously terrifies the reader.

For all secondary characters, such as love interests or bonding characters, it is very rare for an entire curve to be seen onscreen or on the page. However, the writer should be aware of each character's curve even if it doesn't make it on to the page/screen. In *The Wizard of Oz*, we didn't see the Scarecrow get stuck up on the post where Dorothy found him, but we know it was a major motivator for his desire to get a brain (his goal). In *Chicago*, we don't quite see why Velma Kelly is fighting for fame, but we get her resting period (life on the road with her sister and husband) told to us through song. In *Dr. Horrible's Sing Along Blog*, we don't know what event motivated Penny to save the building to use as a homeless shelter, but it's very clear this is her goal.

The best Curve I've ever seen developed for a secondary character came in the film *The Princess Bride*. Inigo Montoya's entire curve is clear, and all of the elements are presented through backstory or on screen. In a compelling monologue only Mandy Patinkin could pull off, Inigo tells us his resting period (life in Spain with his father), inciting incident (his father's death), goal (kill the six fingered man) and rising action up to that point in the story (become a master swordsman and try to find his father's murderer). His goal of avenging his father motivates his every action, including helping to bring Westley back from the dead. We experience his crisis when the six fingered man gets the drop on him and almost kills him ("You've been chasing me your whole life only to fail now? I think that's about the worst thing I've ever heard."). When Inigo rallies and finds the strength to defeat Count Rugen, we are all ecstatic for his victory because we have experienced his entire struggle. It is because we get to experience Inigo's entire Curve that he has one of the most memorable lines in movie history: "Hello. My name is Inigo Montoya. You killed my father. Prepare to die."

Regardless of whether you want to include the entire Curve of secondary characters like Inigo or not, it is essential that all points of the Curve be included for the protagonist. When a reader or viewer opens a book or watches a film, he or she experiences the world through that leading character. This Curve does what a basic plot outline cannot do – it provides a focus on your characters' actions that keeps the story moving, even when the plot starts to lag.

In the next few chapters, I will break down each of these moments of the Major Dramatic Curve and give you very specific examples of how each element is used in a variety of narratives. As you read, think about how you have consciously or unconsciously included each of these elements into your own writing and see if making some small adjustments to your characters' Curves could make massive improvements in how your writing is received.

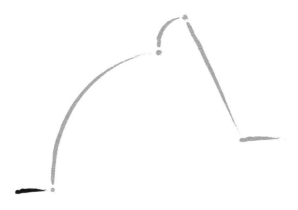

Chapter 5
Resting Period

The first element of the Major Dramatic Curve is the initial place of rest (or Resting Period) of the protagonist. By definition, the Resting Period is the character in their world before their world changes. In some circles, this Resting Period is called the Ordinary World, and for good reason. This is the time when the protagonist is going about her or his daily life. In many ways, this day should be like any other day for the protagonist, except for one huge difference – before too long, something is going to happen to change that person's life forever. That change will wind up the being the main plot for the rest of the story.

In order for people to experience the stories of others, they need to be allowed into the character's world. The Resting Period is the front door through which we walk to enter that world, the introduction to the character and the world before the character's life is uprooted.

And yes, the character's life should be uprooted by the events of the story. If not, then why are we reading the story? What makes the narrative time period more interesting than the year before or the year after? Why tell this particular story? Why focus on these events? If the events aren't important enough to change the protagonist's life forever, then they probably aren't important enough to use as the focal point of a novel, short story, movie or play.

Regardless of whether we are talking about a novel, a film, or a short story, when we enter the world of a narrative, we always want to start at the beginning. This might sound like an obvious and rather over-simplified concept, but many students want to argue with this simple idea. They want to begin in the middle of the story ("in medias res"), allowing the reader or viewer to immediately get thrust into the action.

I understand why more and more students are interested in this kind of storytelling. As various forms of media become popular, they effect storytelling methods, and both television and gaming are famous for starting their stories in an action packed place. With television, it is rather common to see a television show open in a place of action – maybe an exciting fistfight or with a gunshot that seems to kill off a beloved character. Then the action will cut back in time, and the viewer learns what happened "six hours earlier" or "two days earlier." In other words after they see the exciting event, they start the story once more, this time from the beginning. So, while it might look like television starts in the middle of the action, they don't actually skip the beginning of the story. However, the novice writer doesn't always realize this is the case, and they might choose to "ignore" the fact that these shows flash back to the beginning in an effort to support their own decision to eliminate the beginning portion of their own stories.

A great example of this kind of storytelling can be seen in several seasons of the award winning AMC serial *Breaking Bad*. Season One opens with a pair of pants flying into the air, and then a beat up RV running over them. The RV cascades down a desert road, and viewers have no idea where it's going or why a Hawaiian shirt hangs from the rearview mirror. The action then cuts inside where the driver of the RV is revealed. He's stripped to his underwear and wearing a gas mask. Unconscious on the seat next to him is a younger man, also wearing a gas mask. In the back are two seemingly dead bodies. When the driver's mask fogs, he crashes the RV. He hears approaches sirens and begins to panic. He quickly pulls out a video camera and records a heartfelt good-bye to his family. It is at this time we learn his name is Walter White, and that he is a loving father and husband. He then pulls out a gun and gets ready for the oncoming police. At this point, the audience is completely hooked. We want to see the showdown between the police and this strange, half naked man. But then the show cuts back to "Three Weeks Earlier," and what comes next is the beginning. We get to meet Walter and his family before he ever gets involved in any kind of criminal activity. And, most importantly, we have to watch the entire season to get back to that exciting opening.

Season Two of the show is similar, although it opens with a simple image of a pink child's toy in an otherwise black and white pool. At first, we only see the eyeball of the toy and assume it's a human eyeball getting sucked into the pool filter, but then the camera dives deep into the pool where we see the rest of the child's toy. For anyone who watched season one, we know that Walter's children mean everything to him, and so we are anxious to see whose child might be dead. Again, it takes us the rest of the season to find out since the action then cuts back to the final scene of season one. Here, we are able to find out how Walter's life is going to be thrown off balance once again.

The motivating factor behind this popular way of opening television shows is obvious – it results in more viewers. Before the days of DVR and On Demand viewing, television stations had one opportunity to catch viewers – in the first five minutes of their show. They needed to hook viewers right away or lose them. If a viewer didn't like what they saw, they could easily switch the channel and see what they could find that looked "more interesting." In those days, you could only watch one thing at a time, and so you made your choices carefully. Now that viewers can record multiple shows or watch one show live and then catch another On Demand, viewers don't have to be so choosey. However, there are now so many choices out there, TV writers still need to grab a viewer from this start of the show to ensure that they keep watching. But notice, on shows with good writing, you will always get to jump back to the beginning to complete the whole story.

The trend of starting in medias res can also be found in the video game world as well. When a player starts a game, they will usually be thrust, headfirst, into some kind of conflict. This is because... well... it's a game. The player wants to play the game, not just sit back and get a bunch of set-up information like backstory. Often, the first gameplay will be a bit simplistic compared to the rest of the game so the player can learn the game mechanics (A button equals jump, shake the remote to make his spin, etc.). As the player learns more skills, the challenges will get more difficult. Because the player wants to jump directly into gameplay, the game writers will often start in the middle of the story in order to maximize the action.

Usually, the "beginning" of the story (backstory, character details, etc.) will be delivered in one of two ways. The most obvious way is through text or "exposition dumps." Basically, the player will encounter either a dialogue exchange or a cut scene (small cinematic scenes embedded within the gameplay) that tells him about his past. A great example here is *Harvester*, a point-and-click game from the late 90s, but which has recently been re-released via Steam. In this game, you play as Steve, a man who has woken up in a strange town with no memory of his life. Over the course of the game, we meet his family and his fiancée, and in a dark twist, find out Steve is actually a serial killer responsible for much of the gore seen throughout the game. Other characters convey this to the player using very explicit dialogue.

A more subtle way of conveying backstory can be via non-dialogue gameplay mechanics such as perks or stats. In other words, what your character starts off with gives us a sense of who they were before the game began. A great example of this can be seen in *Dominion 3: The Awakening*. In this game, the characters' weapons, magic types and equipment slots serve as nods to who the characters were before the game began. Also, subtle choices, like having a character "blind in one eye" nods to a history without explicitly stating the details of the history. We get a sense of the characters' beginning without having to actually experience it.

That's not to say that all games have to start in the middle of the action. Some very well-written games open at the beginning. *Epic Mickey* may as well open with the words "Once Upon A Time." It starts with a cinematic of Mickey sneaking in the workshop of Yen Sid (the wizard from *Fantasia*), who is in the middle of creating a magical cartoon world. After accidentally creating the evil Ink Blot, Mickey escapes the workshop undetected. But shortly afterwards, he gets kidnapped and pulled into the Cartoon Wasteland by the villain he created. Similarly, *The Last of Us* begins on the night that a mutant fungus sweeps through the United States. This fungus attacks its hosts, turning them into a form of zombies. The player's character Joel tries to escape the city with his brother and his twelve-year-old daughter, Sarah. During the exodus, Sarah is shot and dies in Joel's arms. The game then jumps a full twenty years into the future.

While *Epic Mickey* and *The Last of Us* are great examples of games that obviously start at the beginning, there have been too many games that either reference a beginning or ignore it all together for the sake of gameplay. While this method of storytelling can work very effectively in gaming, it has encouraged writers of other mediums to try to start in the middle of the action instead of starting at the beginning.

So why is it important to begin at the beginning? Well, if we want to ignore Aristotle who encouraged us to always have a beginning, middle, and end, then we may want to ask ourselves these questions: Why do we begin reading a book on page one? Why do we show up before the start of a movie? What is the benefit of seeing a play from the opening scene as opposed to taking a seat at intermission?

For me, the answer is simple: I want to know why I should care about the story. Starting in the middle, at the end, or with a later action scene is a gimmick to hook the reader's/viewer's curiosity rather than doing the harder work of hooking/engaging the reader's/viewer's empathy. There are other ways to use curiosity as a hook without having to flash forward/back to another part of the story. For instance, the first episode of the first season of *The West Wing* opens with all the characters receiving an urgent text and dropping whatever they are doing to deal with it. Allison Janney's character 'CJ' even falls off the treadmill. Only when the final character is introduced (and leaves a beautiful woman in bed to go to work) do we learn what the text says: The President of the United States has been in a bicycle accident. By the time we learn this and our curiosity is satisfied, we have been introduced to a unique set of characters. Now, we want to see how each will handle this public relations crisis when the diverse group meets at the office, which just happens to be the White House.

That opening segment of the story – the Resting Period – is a chance for us to get to know the character in a way that we wouldn't know him or her if we started in the middle. Was that super hero just like me or has he always been strong? Was she always so confident or did she have to learn how to love herself? The resting period is a chance for us to see the protagonist as a real life, just-like-me human being before the amazing obstacles land in her path. If I can't see her as a regular human being, then I can't identify with her.

56

The 2012 film *Chronicle* is a great film to look at when it comes to creating identifiable protagonists. *Chronicle* is interesting because we see the rise of a super villain, but we see it from the villain's side and not the hero's. The protagonist, Andrew, is extremely relatable when we first meet him. He is the social outcast who never quite feels like he has a place. His father abuses him, and he has purchased a camera to get proof of the beatings. His cousin Matt is his only friend, but even Matt thinks he needs to change himself in order to be more popular. Once they encounter the strange meteor rocks that give them special powers, we are already rooting for Andrew. We want him to grow and succeed because we have already accepted him as our equal. After he accidentally kills Steve and takes a turn towards darkness, we are still rooting for him. At the end of the film, where we realize that our super hero has become a super villain, we feel pity for him and not fear. We hope that Matt will fly in and save him from himself.

Andrew is relatable for two reasons: for one, he has a good heart. We see him meaning well but never quite succeeding. He loves his mother and wants the best for her, but his alcoholic father keeps him from being present for her as much as he would like. The accident that scars half his body and lands him in the hospital comes as a direct result of his trying to steal money to obtain his mother's medications. While Andrew's father is out looking for his missing son, his mother dies. Andrew has lost everything. While Andrew kills quite a few people in his pursuit for helping his mother, his intention comes from a positive place. This makes audiences relate to him, even if they think his actions are extreme.

Andrew is also relatable because he is an underdog. As a race, humans are often big fans of the oppressed. We want the downtrodden to fight back and come out on top. Bullies make fun of Andrew at school, and his father beats him up at home. He can't win no matter where he goes. This makes us want to see Andrew fight back and stand up for himself. As humans, we have all felt oppressed at some time, and it is easy to relate to someone else in that same position.

If we didn't relate to Andrew, then his story would be much different. We would see his monologue about the "apex predator" as terrifying instead of invigorating. Once he gets his powers, if we didn't identify with him, we would immediately want him to be stopped, not for him to succeed. That's why it's extremely important for us to get a sense of who he is before he gets his powers.

The Resting Period is the place in any narrative where we get to see that pre-powers aspect of any character. Who are they before their world is thrown out of whack? Why should we care about them? Why are they just like us? When a writer opens a story after the protagonist has left their Ordinary World, then we don't really get to learn this information.

Here are a few other famous protagonists and their Resting Periods:

Protagonist: Mikey – *The Goonies*
Resting Period: Mikey in his home, reluctantly trying to accept that he will have to move. He's a good kid with strong loyalty to his friends, who has a kind yet taunting relationship with his brother.

Protagonist: Frodo – *The Lord of the Rings*
Resting Period: Frodo in the Shire, loving both his life and his uncle. He's innocent and carefree, and the disappearance of his beloved uncle causes him great sadness.

Protagonist: Libby Day – *Dark Places*
Resting Period: Libby has never really gotten over the murders of her past. She labels herself in a way similar to the way others label her – as a victim.

<u>Protagonist</u>: Harry Potter – *Harry Potter and the Philosopher's/ Sorcerer's Stone*

<u>Resting Period</u>: Forced to live in a cupboard under the stairs, Harry receives constant abuse from his aunt, uncle and cousin. As an orphan, he is a boy without a real home or sense of belonging.

<u>Protagonist</u>: Nicholas Angel – *Hot Fuzz*

<u>Resting Period</u>: Nicholas is the top police officer at everything he does. It's clear he is, by far and away, the best PC the London Metropolitan Police Department has ever known.

<u>Protagonist</u>: Dorothy – *The Wizard of Oz*

<u>Resting Period</u>: Dorothy can think of nothing more boring than life on the farm. She dreams of growing up and living life in a more exciting place, far from the livestock and the Mrs. Gulches of the world.

Each of these characters all lack something when we first meet them, and the main events of the story help to fulfill that inner need. We can't truly appreciate what they lack unless we see them before they begin their pursuit of their main goal.

Crafting Your Place of Rest

Think about the protagonist of your story and write out a paragraph summarizing who he or she is in their Ordinary World. As you create this section of your story's Major Dramatic Curve, consider the following tips:

1. Never underestimate the power of a great opening. Whether it's a great first line or a strong visual image, the first thing we see in a narrative helps define the story as a whole. Similarly, what a character is physically doing when we meet

them – their defining action – will also tell us a lot about a character. For example, let's say our protagonist is a well-dressed businessman. If he snorts cocaine when we first meet him, that tells us a lot more about him than if you open your story with him waking up and getting ready for work. As the saying goes, you never get a second chance to make a good first impression, so make sure your protagonist gives a well-defined first impression to your readers/viewers. What would your protagonist's defining action be?

2. All events in the Ordinary World need to be "on screen." In other words, the reader should read about it on the page or the viewer/player needs to see it happen on the screen. No backstory! Your story takes place NOW, so your events should take place now. The backstory can always be added to your narrative later on in the tale. For instance, in *Hot Fuzz*, Nicholas tells us why he became a cop very late in his Rising Action. Harry Potter doesn't learn about the events that made him famous until after his Inciting Incident. Start with the now. You have time to develop the backstory later.

3. Try to make your protagonist identifiable. When we first meet her or him, we should see a piece of ourselves in this person. Even if a character isn't likable, give him a moment that makes us still identify with him. A bully can be abused by an angry parent at home. A grumpy man can keep a child from getting run over. Blake Snyder refers to this moment as a "Save the Cat" moment. By showing your protagonist doing something slightly redeeming or making him/her some kind of underdog, we will immediately identify with him/her, even if they aren't likeable people.

4. Disney also likes to include an "I want" song during the Place of Rest. Here, the characters bluntly state their inner need/

emotional motivation through song. Ariel wants to be "Part of [the human] world." Aladdin doesn't want to be seen as a "riff raff, street rat." Anna wants to connect with her sister, even if it's only to "build a snowman." For non-musical writers, we can turn the "I want" song into an "I wish" statement. The character can bluntly say or do an action that implies their inner emotional need. This way, you set up your emotional need in the Ordinary World, which allows for us to understand what motivates the protagonist once the Inciting Incident arrives. What would your protagonist's "I wish" statement be?

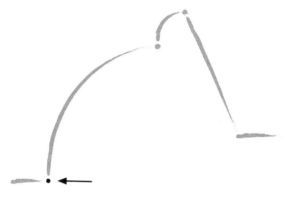

Chapter 6
The Inciting Incident

Once you have established your protagonist's Resting Place, then it is time to throw the Ordinary World out of whack. We do this with the Inciting Incident.

By definition, the Inciting Incident is the external event that launches a protagonist after her or his goal. Keep in mind, the definition reads "the *external* event." The character can't just wake up one morning and decide to go on a quest. She can't just say, "hey, you know what I would really like to try to do today..." and then begin fighting for her goal. He can't just randomly decide that today, of all days, is the day to change his life forever. Something must enter from the outside world and force him or her to begin the uphill battle towards winning the goal.

Screenwriter Michael Arndt refers to the inciting incident as something that threatens a character's happiness. For example, at the beginning of the first *Toy Story*, we meet Woody. In his Resting Place, Woody is established as Andy's favorite toy. This defines him and makes him worthwhile. However, the inciting incident is the arrival of Andy's "new favorite toy" Buzz Lightyear.

Buzz's very arrival in the bedroom threatens Woody's place as Andy's favorite toy, and therefore threatens Woody's happiness as a whole.

In *The Proposal*, Margaret is a successful executive editor-in-chief at a publishing company. She's known for being a savvy yet bossy businesswoman, and she loves her life. She loves being in charge and having the power to put people in their place. When her bosses her tell she must leave the country due to visa issues, her happiness is threatened. It is the desperation created by this threat that pushes her into blackmailing her assistant into marrying her for a green card.

In *The Lord of the Rings: The Fellowship of the Ring* (book), Frodo Baggins loves his life in the Shire. He is innocent and friendly. Even though his uncle's sudden disappearance saddens him, he settles quickly and happily into his new life at Bag End. It isn't until the Shire (the symbol of his happiness and innocence throughout the books) is threatened before he sets out with his three mates to bring the One Ring to Rivendell. Keep in mind, he doesn't just decide to leave his life when Bilbo disappears because, as much as he loved his uncle, he wasn't the source of Frodo's happiness. When Gandalf tells him he must take the Ring to the elves, it is the threat to the Shire that launches Frodo out the door.

Similarly, in *Pride and Prejudice*, Elizabeth Bennett's happiness is threatened by the rather insulting remarks of Mr. Darcy. Normally happy and carefree, hearing him refer to her as "tolerable" and "slighted by other men" impacted her otherwise pleasant evening. This "shocking rudeness" greatly influences her every other action in the book as she tries to get her subtle revenge on the rich Dr. Darcy.

Sometimes, the "happiness" upset by the inciting incident can't quite by seen as "happiness." In these cases, "contentment" might be a better word. At the beginning of *Dark Places*, protagonist Libby Day can't be called happy – not by a long shot. Growing up as the famous, lone survivor of a mass homicide at her family home, she's become comfortable in her place playing the victim. She's a neurotic mess with no real interpersonal connections. She has a cat but she rarely remembers to feed it. She has become completely dependent on her identity as the survivor of the "The Satan Sacrifice of Kinnakee, Kansas." Unable and unwilling to hold down a job, even her income is based on her victim status. When her lawyer tells her that the money she accumulated after the murders is completely gone and she must find a way to support herself, her victim status is now threatened. This is her inciting incident because the life she has come to accept can no longer continue to exist.

Similarly, *The Hunger Games'* Katniss Everdeen isn't exactly happy at the beginning of the first book. However, she has found a comfortable place as her family's stand-in matriarch. Since her father is dead, her mother is one step above catatonic, and her sister is helpless, Katniss has stepped up to be the guiding figure in her family. Each day, she hunts illegally in order to keep food on her family's table. While you can't exactly call her happy, she has come to terms with this position. When her sister's name is called at the Reaping (her inciting incident), her position as family savior has been threatened. In order to fight for her family, she has no choice but to volunteer as tribute.

Don't get the wrong idea; Inciting incidents aren't all bad. Sometimes, the "threat" to happiness isn't that happiness will be taken away. Sometimes, the protagonist can be confronted with some opportunity for their happiness to be secured. In *The Goonies*, Mikey has come to terms with the unhappy news that he must move to a new community. His neighborhood will be destroyed by a local country club making a new golf course, and so he must say farewell to his lifelong friends. But when they find the old treasure map in his father's attic (inciting incident), he realizes he might not have to accept defeat after all. He has one last chance to do what his parents couldn't: save his neighborhood by finding One Eyed Willy's treasure.

Harry Potter also experiences a similar opportunity for happiness in his inciting incident. When Hagrid arrives at the falling down shack in which his foster parents have attempted to hide him, Harry discovers his life means more than he was originally led to believe. Harry is a wizard whose parents died, not in a car accident, but in a heroic fashion. Now, Harry has the opportunity to prove that he isn't the loser orphan his aunt, uncle and cousin said he was.

Hamlet, too, finds himself confronted with the ability to reject his current lifestyle. At the beginning of the play, Hamlet is disgusted by his mother and uncle's wedding because he thinks it's too soon after his father's death. When Horatio brings him to his father's ghost, the resentment he felt against his mother for marrying too quickly after his father's death is compounded by the fact that this new husband is also the murderer of his father. The ghost has tempted Hamlet with an offer he can't refuse – to seek vengeance against the man who murdered his beloved father.

The inciting incident has upset the "normal" or "Ordinary" world of the protagonist. This makes the events that follow matter. We want to see the protagonist bring his world back into balance, and that is why readers and viewers stay tuned (to continue to read or watch) the rest of the story.

It is easy to see how the Resting Place and the Inciting Incident are interconnected. Without having a chance to see the protagonist in their place of happiness or contentment, we can't really understand why the change at the end has affected them so completely. Similarly, without seeing that external event which inspires them to action, we can't really appreciate the lives they had before the change. These two pieces are essential to master, not only because of how they work together but because they are at the beginning of the story.

Crafting Your Inciting Incident

Write out a paragraph in which you explore your inciting incident and the effect it has on your protagonist. As you create this section of your story's Major Dramatic Curve, consider the following tips:

1. It's important to ask one big question about your inciting incident: why now? An inciting incident needs to have importance and be a once-in-a-lifetime event that ultimately changes the character at his/her core. Therefore, it can't be something mundane. Ask yourself why the events happen when they happen. Could it have happened a week earlier or later? If so, then rethink the events surrounding your story to make the Inciting Incident a result of a perfect storm of well-timed events. This is why so many of our modern stories take place around last pinnacle life effects: the cop who has to solve his hardest case just before he retires, the disappearance of his wife on their fifth wedding anniversary, the last party before the students go off to various colleges, etc. What's the timely importance of your inciting incident?

2. The inciting incident needs to immediately result in a character fighting for his or her goal. This means a long stretch of time can't pass between an inciting incident and the beginning of the Rising Action. If a character's inciting incident is the murder of a parent, then character needs to immediately seek revenge unless we are told the character fought for her or his goal when we weren't present. Inigo Montoya tells us he trained for years to be a master swordsman in order to avenge his father's death. How much time passes between your Inciting Incident and your character's fight to win a goal? If there is a gap of hours, days, weeks, months or years, then why does that gap exist? Why did the character wait so long to start their journey? And why did they start it when they did? Why not the week before or the week after?

Chapter 7
Rising Action

The Rising Action is the meat and potatoes of any story, and it tends to be the material the viewer or reader most remembers. By definition, the Rising Action is the protagonist's uphill struggle to win her/his goal. This is the interplay of tactics and obstacles that make up the meal of the narrative.

Tactics

During this period, the protagonist will do anything to win that goal. In writing terms, we refer to all the ways a character attempts to win the goal as tactics. A well-written character won't just try one thing to win the goal; they will try any number of combinations of items until they discover the one that works best.

In his pursuit to save the Shire, Frodo Baggins not only takes the One Ring to Rivendell, but he later agrees to take the Ring all the way to Mount Doom so it can be destroyed. He agrees to have friends accompany him in his pursuit of his goal when it is helpful (Sam, Merry, Pippin, etc) but he is also willing to part with them when it is not (Boromir, Aragorn, etc). He puts on the Ring when he needs to hide, and he offers it to Galadriel when he thinks she can protect his world better than he could. All he cares about is protecting the Shire, and he will do anything he must in order to win that goal, even if it means accepting his own death at the end of the trilogy.

In *Gone Girl*, Nick does whatever he can to get his wife, Amy, returned to him and, in turn, not go to jail for murder. He cooperates with the police, investigates some of Amy's past stalkers, hires an over-priced attorney, and even admits to his year-long affair on national television. Once he realizes Amy has staged her own disappearance, he lies on television in an attempt to manipulate her to returning to him. He'll do anything he can to get her back: first because he doesn't want any harm to come to her, and later because he wants to kill her himself.

In *The Wizard of Oz*, Dorothy blindly follows the advice of anyone who tells her how she might get home. When the Munchkins tell her to follow the yellow brick road to find the Wizard, she agrees. On her way, she only befriends the Tin Man, The Scarecrow and the Cowardly Lion because she believes they can help her on her journey, and, at the same time, she can help them. In the end, trusting them to help her pays off. Once the Wizard tells her he will only help her if she brings him the broomstick of the Wicked Witch of the West, her three friends are the only ones who can save her from the Witch's murderous rage and flying monkeys.

The key thing to remember about choosing tactics for a character is that you must allow your characters to be selfish. When it comes to fighting for a goal, all characters should be selfish, even if they aren't otherwise selfish people. For them, whatever they want should feel like it's a life or death situation.

They should be desperate to win, and it is this selfishness that will change them on a fundamental level. They will be willing to do things they would not otherwise have done because of their desire to win their goal.

In the novel *Dark Places*, Libby Day only reveals her secrets to the Kill Club, and later comes face to face with the truth of the past, because she needs money. Mikey's pursuit of the treasure drives him to give the motivating speech that prevents the other Goonies from going up "Troy's bucket," an act that would have assured the safety of their lives. Wreck-It Ralph only befriends the obnoxious and rude Vanellope in order to get back the medal she used to gain entry into the big race. The overall plot of each of these stories is a direct result of the tactics each character uses in order to win their goal.

The tactics a character uses to win her or his goal should be rooted in the unique personality you have created for that character. Let's say, for example, you have a scene that takes place on a playground. One child has stolen another child's toy, and the second child's goal is to get that toy back. If the child trying to retrieve her toy is an innocent who believes others can help her, then she might run off to a teacher. However, if the child has learned, even at their young age, that adults can't be trusted, then the child might kick and bite at the other child in order to get the toy back. This is why, when Draco Malfoy steals Neville Longbottom's remembrall, Harry immediately jumps on his broom to get it back whereas Hermione scolds him, reminding him of their teacher's threat of expulsion.

No choice of tactic should be obvious or stereotypical. Don't default to assuming a character will react to a stimulus in a given way because that is the way "everyone reacts to it." No one but loyal-to-her-friends Dorothy would have thrown water on the Scarecrow to put out the fire on his arm, inadvertently melting the Wicked Witch of the West. No one but Mikey would have allowed Andie to think he was his brother so he could experience that first kiss. Only Elizabeth Bennett would walk through the mud for miles to reach her sick sister. We are even told that Katniss Everdeen is the first volunteer tribute from District Twelve. These are well-conceived tactics that the writer has included as a reflection of the individual characters.

Even if two characters want the same thing, they can use different tactics in order to achieve the same goal. In the movie *National Treasure*, Ben Gates (Nicolas Cage) and Ian Howe (Sean Beam) both want to find the long-lost treasure of the Templar Knights but Ian is willing to kill for it, whereas Ben is not. Think about how both men attempted to steal the Declaration of Independence: Ben snuck into a party and used intelligence and technology to bypass security. Ian, however, broke into the facility, knocked out a guard and even fired bullets at the Declaration. These varying tactics were direct results of the individual personalities of the characters.

As the story progresses, the tactics a character uses should become more daring and desperate. A character that would never consider committing murder, for example, might grow to that level of desperation late in the story. Someone who would never abandon their children might do just that in order to succeed. Elizabeth Bennett throws decorum aside and chides Mr. Darcy after she discovers it was his fault her sister is unmarried. As the cave crashes down around them, Mikey is ready to throw his life away and go back for the treasure instead of swim for safety. Libby Day, once unwilling to touch her past at all, walks willingly into the home of her brother's ex-girlfriend, narrowly escaping with her life as she tries to learn the truth. Wreck-It Ralph destroys Vanellope's racing car in order to fulfill the deal with King Candy that gave him back his medal. These characters all must grow into their own worst enemies by the time story is done.

Obstacles

If all the characters had to do was fight selfishly for their goals, the story wouldn't be very interesting. Something needs to stand in the way of the characters' and their desperate tactics. These are called obstacles. Obstacles are external and internal events that stand in the way of the protagonist winning his or her goal. They can stand in the way directly, or they can thwart an individual tactic the protagonist was trying to use in order to win that goal.

Harry Potter faces many obstacles in his pursuit to prove himself at Hogwarts. Draco Malfoy, Severus Snape and even Voldemort are characters who serve as obstacles standing in Harry's way. The trials set-up to guard the Philosopher's Stone (in the book, these include the three-headed dog, the poison bottles, the chess match, etc.) all serve as physical obstacles. But Harry must overcome more conceptual obstacles as well, including his own self-doubt, his lack of knowledge about the Wizarding community and the way that his classmates view him as a result of his past.

In *The Wizard of Oz*, Dorothy's biggest obstacle is that she doesn't know the way home and must rely on other people. In *Toy Story*, Woody has to avoid being seen by humans as he tries to get Buzz back to Andy's bedroom. Everything from orcs to elves to bipolar former Hobbits stand in Frodo's way of saving the Shire. Mikey has to find a treasure that's been missing for centuries with little time to defuse booby-traps because the Goonies are being pursued by the Fratellis. Elizabeth has to operate under a very strict code of behavior expected from young women of her age. All of these characters must overcome these obstacles if they hope to win their goals.

In a good story, there should be at least as many obstacles as there are tactics, plus a few more thrown in for good measure. The obstacles need to be challenging, and we, as a reader or viewer, need to doubt whether or not the protagonist can overcome them. If the obstacles are too easy or if it's too obvious what tactics they will use to win, we will lose interest in the story and respect in the character. We will say, "Why didn't she just call the police when she knew her sister was kidnapped?" or "Why didn't he just use the money to leave town?"

Readers want the characters they fall in love with to really need to work hard for their goals, otherwise, they don't feel like the ending is "earned." I've seen so many films and read so many books where the characters get a happy ending, but they really didn't deserve it. Usually, this happens as a result of a "dues ex machina." Literally translated, this term means "machine of the Gods" or "Gods from the machine." A more modern day translation is "the hand of God." This expression comes from ancient Greek theater where sometimes, when a character is really in trouble, the Gods will swoop down and smite the villain – just because they want to. Therefore, the hero wins but not because of anything they did on their own. They won their goal, but they didn't earn it.

For many years, Stephen King had a reputation for not writing the endings of his story very well, and one of those endings happens to have a great example of dues ex machina. In *The Stand*, mankind struggles to survive in the wake of a terrible plague after it has wiped out most of the planet. In the United States, all of the "good" people have gathered together in Boulder, Colorado, whereas all the "evil" people have gathered in – where else? – Las Vegas, Nevada, under the direction of the Crimson King, Randall Flagg. Over the course of the book, Flagg's people obtain a nuclear warhead. Their plans of launching this warhead to take out the "Free Zone" in Boulder is thwarted when – quite literally – the hand of God drops down from the heavens and detonates the nuke in the middle of the downtown Las Vegas, killing all of Flagg's army. The build up to this 900 page ensemble piece is thrilling, and we are rooting for good to destroy evil. And in a way, it does, but not in a satisfying way. The reader (or watcher of the mini-series) feels cheated by this underdeveloped ending that works on a thematic level but not in terms of character.

While not quite so obvious as The Stand, the ending of *The Goonies* also feels a bit like a dues ex machina. Mikey and his friends were forced to ditch the treasure they found when the Fratellis show up on the pirate ship. When the cave begins to collapse, and they are forced to flee without the gold, it feels like our heroes have lost their goal of saving their community. They have undoubtedly changed as people, and we respect the journey they have gone on. This respect gets a bit tarnished however, when the very random ending takes us in a new direction. For some odd reason, the owner of the country club shows up on the beach asking for the final signature, ensuring the neighborhood's demise. Then, the Spanish speaking maid finds an assortment of jewels in Mikey's jacket pocket. "It's my marble bag. The Fratellis forgot to check it." *Forgot?* The viewer is happy for this turn of events, but it doesn't quite feel like an earned win for the protagonist. A much more satisfying ending would have been if "Mouth" had been successful in his tactic of trying to sneak out the jewels in his mouth.

The device of the Dues Ex Machina is used so often in modern storytelling that the 2004 film *Dodgeball: A True Underdog Story* even plays with it to enhance their comedy. In the film, Peter La Fleur owns a struggling gymnasium frequented by an eccentric group of losers. To save their gym, they form a dodgeball team who come together to compete in the National Dodgeball Tournament. In an act of desperation, Peter sells his gym to his competitor White Goodman. At this point, he thinks his team has no chance of winning, and he thinks his gym is as good as gone anyway. He almost leaves the city before a pep talk by a celebrity cameo convinces him to go back and play. Peter's team rallies to win the National Dodgeball Competition, but since he has already sold his gym, it looks like it was all for naught. However, at the last moment, the casino sweeps in with a treasure chest full of money, congratulating him for his gambling winnings. It is revealed that Peter took the money he received from White and gambled it on his own team winning the Competition. This money allows Peter to not only save his gym but to buy out White's gym as well. Written on the side of the Treasure Chest filled with money are the words "Dues Ex Machina," which shows the screenwriters knew they were ending the film on a cheap trick that would ensure a happy, albeit unearned, ending.

To avoid these cheap, unearned endings, the obstacles of the Rising Action should get harder and harder. Make things difficult, but not impossible. Screw your characters, but not yourself. At the beginning of the narrative, the protagonist should not possess the skills he or she needs to overcome all of these obstacles. However, as the protagonist experiments with various tactics, he or she learns skills or knowledge that will result in his or her ability to beat out the final obstacle in the end.

Just be sure the lessons the character learns aren't too close to the obstacle that it is used to overcome. We want the reader/viewer to almost forget about the lesson until it's important for the character to use it later on. For instance, in *Monty Python and The Holy Grail*, King Arthur learns there are two different kinds of swallows in the beginning of the movie. This knowledge seems just like another bit of absurd silliness at the time. The audience laughs but forgets about this joke. Later, however, when King Arthur uses that knowledge to pass one of the final obstacles toward the end of the film, the audience remembers and laughs instead of groans.

As writers, it is important to realize there are two levels to this interplay of tactics and obstacles: one for each scene and one for the narrative overall. Within each scene, the character needs to have a goal for that scene. To win that goal, they need to have a number of various obstacles they must overcome.

This scene goal is, in turn, a tactic towards winning their larger, narrative long goal.

A great example can be seen in *Harry Potter and the Goblet of Fire* (book). His goal is to survive the newest threat from Voldemort. This starts at the Quidditch World Cup and ends when Dumbledore prevents Barty Crouch Jr. from murdering Harry in the Defense Against the Dark Arts office. As Harry journeys through his pursuit of his goal, he encounters multiple tasks. One of these tasks is the hedge maze, in the middle of which the Triwizard Cup is hidden. His scene goal is to get to the Cup. Some of the tactics he uses to win this goal are to run through the maze, to solve the Sphinx's riddle, to avoid the Blast Ended Skrewt and to avoid his competitors, one of who happens to be controlled by the Imperius Curse. His obstacles in this scene are the various magical creatures and spells he comes across, his fellow competitors, his own fear, his inability to leave an unconscious competitor behind, and — though he doesn't know – it a Death Eater who has turned the Cup into a transportation device which will deliver him directly into the hands of Voldemort. Overall, his scene goal of getting to the Cup is a tactic towards his overall goal. Winning that Cup will end the Triwizard Tournament, which is the most obvious threat against him. His other overall tactics are similar in nature: passing the Underwater Challenge, getting the golden egg from the Dragon Challenge, and, of course, surviving the Yule Ball.

As you approach writing your Rising Action, it's important you keep in mind the relationship between those scene goals and the overall goal. In a well-crafted story, those pieces should work together to form the overall story. If a scene goal does not, in some way, contribute to the overall goal, then perhaps that scene isn't needed and can be eliminated. Similarly, if you find one scene goal is reached too easily, then perhaps more obstacles need to be added to help increase the overall difficulty of the character winning his or her goal. All of these pieces should fit together nicely, creating a solid build as you move into the last two elements of the Major Dramatic Curve: the crisis and the climax.

Crafting Your Rising Action

Instead of writing a paragraph for the Rising Action, write a two column chart: obstacles in the left column, tactics in the right column. As you write, consider these tips:

1. Your tactics and obstacles should usually talk to each other. For example, a character's goal is to save a princess from a dragon. The obstacles can include a) the dragon's cave is in a hard to reach place, b) the dragon breaths fire, and c) the princess is chained to the wall. The tactics speaking directly to these obstacles can include a) the protagonist hires an expert mountain climber to help him, b) the protagonist wears a fire-proof safety uniform, and c) the protagonist goes out and learns how to pick a padlock. Make sure you don't introduce an obstacle the protagonist never deals with.

2. You should always have more tactics than obstacles. Your reader/viewer wants to see the protagonist try some things that fail before they succeed. Otherwise, how does the protagonist learn?

3. Make your obstacles as hard as possible. Ask yourself this question: what's the one thing that would make it impossible for my character to win his goal? Then add that to your obstacle list. For example, in *National Treasure*, Ben steals the Declaration of Independence. His goal is to get the Templar treasure. If he got arrested for stealing the Declaration, there is no way he could get the treasure. So what happens? The FBI catch him and arrest him. In *Gone Girl*, Nick wants his wife Amy to return. What would

be the worst thing that could happen? If Amy actually got killed or kidnapped while she was out on her own. So what happens? Amy calls a creep friend who takes her to his lake house, where she becomes his prisoner. Make it impossible for your character to win their goal, and then find a way for them to get around that obstacle. This way, your audience respects the journey they have gone through and the obstacles they have overcome.

4. Take a look at your tactics and ask this question: are your characters becoming increasingly desperate as the story unfolds? Are there things your character is willing to do later in the narrative they weren't willing to do earlier? If not, why not? As the character grows more desperate, the reader/viewer will feel the intensity they are going through.

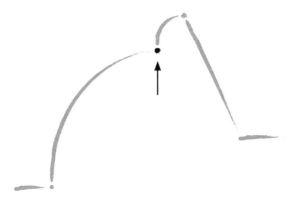

Chapter 8
Crisis Point

As the protagonist approaches his or her goal, using tactics to overcome obstacles along the way, the reader's investment in the character's struggle increases. As the protagonist experiences the rises and falls of their journey, the reader/viewer too rides the same emotional roller coaster. This emotional parallel most strongly exists at the next stop on the Major Dramatic Curve: the Crisis Point.

The Crisis Point is a difficult element to define because, depending on the genre in which you write, it is something very different. In some stories, it can be an emotional low for the character. In others, it can be the character's happiest moment. One thing is very clear about this moment, though; the Crisis Point serves as an indicator that the protagonist has reached his or her greatest challenge (biggest obstacle) and the journey towards their goal will be ending soon.

There are three basic ways that a Crisis Point can appear in any given narrative. It can be an emotional peak (highest/lowest moment), a crossroads where the character must make a difficult decision regarding their goal, or a final piece of information that solves a problem for the protagonist. In all cases, the Crisis Point tends to be a Point of No Return for the protagonist. Once they have experienced this event, there is no way they can go back to who they were at the beginning of the story.

Crisis Point As Emotional Peak

The first kind of Crisis Point is an emotional peak. To explore this kind of Crisis Point, let's look at the traditional definitions of comedy and tragedy. The traditional definition of comedy is much different than how we use the word today. While today a comedy must make us laugh, in traditional terms, a comedy was a narrative with a happy ending. This usually meant that the protagonist won his or her goal. It also usually meant the happiness was sealed with a marriage or marriage proposal. Conversely, a tragedy, in the traditional sense, usually ends with the protagonist losing his or her goal. In many instances, this character usually has a place of authority or control that they lose as a result of their character flaws (such as pride). Today, we tend to think of a tragedy as a story that makes us sad, regardless of whether or not the protagonist wins the goal. However, in the traditional sense, the character must lose their goal in order for the term "tragedy" to be applied.

To look at Crisis Point as an emotional peak, we will use those traditional definitions of comedy and tragedy to indicate what kind of emotional peak the character will experience. In a comedy (character wins the goal), the Crisis Point will be a low point for the character. In a tragedy (character loses the goal), the Crisis Point will be a highest moment for the character. (Sounds a little backwards, doesn't it? Read on...)

When the emotional peak is a lowest moment for the character, the protagonist often feels completely abandoned and destitute. Due to the events that brought about this lowest moment, the protagonist usually thinks there is no way to win the goal. The reader/viewer should also feel this way. In *The Town*, Doug MacRay wants nothing more than to abandon his life of crime and protect the woman he loves. But at his lowest moment, the seedy crime boss and florist Fergie Colm has blackmailed him. He must participate in the most dangerous robbery of his career or the crime boss will murder Claire, Doug's girlfriend. Fergie has also destroyed Doug's innocent belief that his mother is alive somewhere. She was a drug addict who killed herself thanks to Fergie. On top of this, the FBI is on to Doug and has alerted Claire of his true identity. When he runs to Claire's house to convince her to run away with him, she threatens to call the police. She's terrified of him and wants nothing more to do with him. Doug has lost everything in this moment. He feels completely trapped. He can't escape his life of crime or else the woman he loves will die. This is his lowest moment and Crisis Point.

In *Pride and Prejudice*, Elizabeth Bennett suffers her emotional low when Lydia and Wickham run off together. Not only has her sister ruined the entire family's reputation, but it has seemingly also ruined Elizabeth's chances for receiving a second proposal of marriage from Mr. Darcy. Before this time, Darcy and Elizabeth reconciled at Pemberley, and his actions were so affectionate and caring that Elizabeth believed she might once again have a chance. However, Darcy runs off almost as soon as he learns about the elopement. Elizabeth returns to her home, convinced that she and her beloved three sisters will never be able to marry.

In *Harry Potter and the Goblet of Fire*, Harry's Crisis Point comes in the form of Voldemort's resurrection. Not only is Harry as far away from winning the Triwizard Tournament as possible, but now his blood has assisted the worst wizard of all time to return to full power. As a result, Voldemort has acquired the protection spell Harry's mother cast over him as a baby. Harry literally accepts his own death, telling himself that he will die fighting like his father instead of cowering behind a gravestone. Things can't get much blacker than it does for Harry in that chapter in the graveyard.

The lowest point for these characters usually results from the character being faced with their largest obstacle and feeling like they are losing. They are ready to give up all together, throw in the towel and cut their losses if they can. However, since these are all comedies in the traditional sense, the fight isn't over for them just yet. Something will inspire them to pick themselves up by their bootstraps and fight one more epic battle towards winning their goal. Doug participates in the robbery of Fenway Park, narrowly escaping with his life, murdering the florist, finding a moment of reconciliation with Claire and then escaping to Florida. Elizabeth and her family are delighted to learn that Lydia was married. After this, she urges her father to accept them in the house to avoid scandal, encourages her sister's reconciliation with Mr. Bingley, stands up to Lady Catherine de Bourgh's threats and accepts Mr. Darcy's wedding proposal. Through a stroke of magical luck, Harry and Voldemort's wand connect, conjuring the ghost of Harry's parents who help him escape the graveyard. Harry then fights to overcome the final foe in the book: Barty Crouch Jr. before finally returning to the comfort of his friends. For all of these characters, their lowest moments didn't defeat them, and we, as reader/viewers, respect them for not succumbing to those lowest moments.

When looking at tragedies, the Crisis Points look very different. Since the characters are going to lose their goal, the Crisis Point is the moment where it looks like nothing could go wrong for them. They are on top of the world, and only an act of God could remove them from their place of privilege. In the most well known tragedy of all time, King Lear reunites with his beloved daughter Cordelia. Even though Lear disowned her, she showers him with nothing but love. On top of that, she and the King of France have an entire army ready to mount an attack against her evil sisters. At this point in the play, it looks like everything will be okay for the pride-filled king. This is his highest moment and Crisis Point.

In the television show *Breaking Bad*, Walter White experiences an emotional high for his Crisis Point. Since the entire five seasons of the show are all one continuous storyline, we can consider his entire story as one large Major Dramatic Curve. His Crisis Point comes at the end of Season Four. His plan of using Gus Fring's long time nemesis against him has worked. Fring is killed in the nursing home explosion, and Walt and his associate Jesse have burned the meth lab to the ground, destroying all evidence of his involvement. It is at this point of his story where Walt literally says "I won." It looks like he could completely walk away from the drug industry, his family safe from harm.

In the second book of *The Hunger Games*, *Catching Fire*, Katniss seems to be well on her way of winning her goal to protect Peeta. The other tributes have rallied around her, and they have figured out the main puzzle of the current Hunger Games. She and Peeta sit comfortably on the beach, feeling as safe as anyone possibly could while being in the Games. They plan to escape the other tributes and hope they can outlive them all. At this moment, Katniss's high point isn't enviable but it's the most joy she experiences in her journey.

After these emotional highs, each of these tragic protagonists then finds their journey towards their goal spiraling out of control. In *King Lear*, Cordelia is murdered, and Lear dies of a broken heart. Walter White can't give up his life as a meth-making kingpin and winds up destroying his entire family, and Katniss destroys the Games Arena but loses her goal of protecting Peeta when the Capitol captures him. To add insult to injury, Katniss's entire District is then bombed off the face of the earth. They have all fallen from a place of assumed success into darkness.

Regardless of whether you are writing a comedy or a tragedy, the important thing to remember about an Emotional Peak Crisis Point is that the characters are lulled into a false sense of their own success or failure. They are either entirely in control of their own fate or entirely sure they can never win their goal. This extreme makes their final journey towards the climax all the more powerful.

Crisis Point as Crossroads

Sometimes, the Crisis Point doesn't appear in such an extreme fashion. If a writer doesn't want a "highest high" or a "lowest low," then the Crisis Point may appear as a kind of crossroads, a difficult decision the protagonist must make. Usually, this decision involves the protagonist having to choose if they want to continue to pursue their original goal or if they want to give up that goal in order to chase a different goal. Many times, this "different goal" becomes a moral decision; in other words, giving up the first goal is done in the name of "doing the right thing."

In the animated film *Wreck-It Ralph*, the protagonist fights to win a medal that he can take back to his game, *Fix-It Felix*, in order to prove he is a good guy. When King Candy gives him the medal, he destroys Vanellope's car. Ralph then returns to *Fix-It Felix* where he discovers his home game has been placed out of order. With Ralph missing, the game didn't work as intended, and the arcade owner assumed it was broken. Having brought the medal back to his game, he receives the penthouse apartment he was promised if he succeeded, but now the Nicelanders (the minor characters of *Fix-It Felix*) have abandoned the game. He is now faced with a choice: find a way to save his own game so he can still prove that he is a good guy or just let his game die and do "the right thing" by going back to help Vanellope. Working to fix his own game would service his original goal of trying to prove himself to his fellow *Fix-It Felix* characters. However, going back and helping Vanellope like he promised is "the right thing to do." Making this difficult decision is his Crisis Point.

Similarly, Frodo must make a difficult decision in *The Lord of the Rings: The Fellowship of the Ring*. While his overall goal of saving the Shire continues throughout the book series, each of the individual narratives has their own Major Dramatic Curve as well. In the first installment, his primary tactic for saving the Shire is to rely on the wisdom and experience of others. He is willing to give the Ring to anyone who might be able to do more good than he deserves he is able to do, including Gandalf, the elves of Rivendell, and Galadriel. After a deranged Boromir tries to take the ring from him, he is faced with the horrible decision of staying with the Fellowship or taking Galadriel's advice and going off alone. On the one hand, Frodo is "just" a hobbit, a race with little experience in worldly matters. Small and unseasoned, the idea of Frodo making it all the way to Mount Doom on his own is ludicrous. Conversely, however, Boromir's attempt to take the Ring acts as evidence to the notion that the journey will destroy them all, especially the human men. Frodo knows finding the courage to go off on his own is the "right thing" to do, but the difficulty of this decision comes from the idea that doing the "right thing" might result in the failure of his mission.

Margaret Tate must make a similar decision in *The Proposal*. Her goal is to stay in the country so she can keep her job, and she has succeeded in convincing her assistant Andrew to marry her. The con has gone over so well, Andrew's family stages a wedding ceremony for them at their family home in Alaska. All Margaret has to do is walk down the aisle, and say "I do." Her goal will be won, and she will be married to the man she has come to fall in love with. Unfortunately, it is because of her feelings for Andrew, she struggles with completing her mission. Dressed and ready to get married, she must make the choice: continue with her goal or do the "right thing" and admit the truth to everyone, including the INS agent ready to deport her.

In each of these cases, the protagonist chooses to do the "right thing" and winds up winning their original goal anyway. In helping Vanellope, Ralph proves he's a hero and is finally accepted by the Nicelanders. By leaving the main party behind, Frodo and Sam are able to sneak into Mordor. Despite some major setbacks along the way, they destroy the Ring and save the world. After returning to the Shire, they overthrow Saruman's men, thereby saving the Shire as well. Margaret chooses to cancel the wedding, but Andrew refuses to let her go. He chases her back to New York where he asks her to marry him so he can have the chance to date her. While not all of these stories are meant to be morality tales, the result of this kind of decision is that the reader/viewer walks away from the story with a conscious or unconscious reinforced belief in the idea that we should always do what is right in order to get the things we want.

Not all crossroad Crisis Points wear such rose-colored glasses. Sometimes, the protagonist makes the wrong decision and then must deal with the consequences. In the first book of Stephen King's *Dark Tower* series, *The Gunslinger's* Crisis Point forces Roland to make a decision that haunts him throughout the rest of the series. On the chase of "the Man in Black", Roland and Jake, a young boy mysteriously transported from our world into Roland's, must journey underground or else lose the trail of the man they seek. During their underground adventure, Jake trips and almost falls off a large drop. Unfortunately for Jake, it is at this moment when the Man in Black appears. Roland has a choice, save Jake and lose the Man in Black forever, or let Jake die and win his goal. Roland leaves Jake to die and finally catches the Man in Black. His goal is won, but the guilt of leaving Jake behind to die resonates with him over the rest of the series.

The Vanishing (both versions of the film) also shows a choice leading to regret. In this film, a man obsessed with finding his wife is faced with a choice. The man who is responsible for her disappearance will show him what happened to his wife, but only if the protagonist drinks a cup of drugged coffee. The protagonist's choice is clear: do the "right thing" by not trusting this man and calling the police or drink the coffee and win his goal. The protagonist, who has a different name in each version of the film, chooses to drink the coffee. He regrets this decision when he wakes up buried alive in a coffin beneath the earth. By not doing the right thing, he wound up dead.

In Ian McEwen's *Atonement,* the true identity of the protagonist isn't really revealed until the very end of the narrative. However, once you know the protagonist is Briony, her crossroad is clear. She had the chance to go to her sister's house and apologize for the stories she told as a child, one of which resulted in Robbie's jailing and eventual death. She could complete her goal of impressing people with her stories or she could do the "right thing" and make up for the sins of her past. Unfortunately, she never found the courage to do the right thing. Forced to make amends through her stories instead of in real life, she refers to her poor attempts at making up for her past as a "final act of kindness." (More about this wonderful narrative will surface in Chapter 12!)

Regardless of whether the protagonist chooses to continue to pursue their goal or to "do the right thing," when a Crisis Point takes the shape of a crossroads decision, it needs to be a huge choice with significant stakes. Just like the Emotional Peak Crisis Point, the Crossroad Crisis Point is a Point of No Return. Once the character has made this tough decision, she or he can never return to who they were at the beginning of the story because their choice has redefined who they are as an individual.

Crisis Point As New Information

When a writer scribes a murder mystery, a thriller or a horror story, they will often need to use a third kind of Crisis Point: the introduction of New Information. This New Information can be actual information (a fact, detail, item) discovered by the protagonist or it can be new information revealed to the reader/viewer. Either way, the new information revealed drastically changes the forward momentum of the story, and the protagonist has no choice but to kill or be killed (literally or figuratively).

In terms of how this kind of Crisis Point is used, most readers/viewers tend to think of the new information revealed to the character. In *Se7en*, Detective Mills learns that John Doe has the upper hand. In *Hot Fuzz*, Nicholas discovers the police chief plus the entire Neighborhood Watch Association are responsible for the string of grisly murders in the small, picture-perfect village. In *The Name of the Rose*, where poisoned ink on a book kills various clergymen, the poisoned book is literally found in a secret room the protagonist never entered until the Crisis Point. Mystery readers are very familiar with this new kind of information presented towards the end of the story that finally gives the detective (or detective figure) the clues he or she needs to solve the case.

But what if the new information takes the form of dramatic irony? In other words, what about the times when the new information is presented to the reader/viewers instead of to the characters within the world of the narrative? A great example of this kind of Crisis Point can be seen in the horror film *Paranormal Activity*. In this film, a young couple begins to film their bedroom each night to discover the strange noises and disruptions occurring in their house while they attempt to sleep. The new information presented in this film's Crisis Point is the kind of information revealed to the viewer and not to the characters. After being pulled out of her bed and into a hallway closet, Katie's character changes dramatically. The Crisis Point comes when it is revealed to the audience that Katie is now possessed. She climbs out of bed and stares menacingly at her husband Micah for hours. For the rest of the film, we want to shout at Micah to get out of the house and run for his life. Unfortunately, we are powerless to do anything but sit back and watch the horror unfold.

When introducing new information as the Crisis Point, it's important for the writer to realize that this information needs to be held back until the last moment. The protagonist needs to do everything in his or her power to win the goal, and it is only when it looks like they are close to failure when this information is revealed.

High-Speed Trajectory

More often than not, a writer will choose to use a Crisis Point in more than one of the above-mentioned capacities. Elizabeth Bennett's lowest moment comes with the difficult decision of doing the right thing and revealing the truth of her sister's indiscretion to Darcy. *Wreck-It Ralph*'s decision to abandon his original goal is partnered with new information about Vanellope. In *The Town*, Doug's lowest moment also forces him to make a choice: flee to Florida and leave the woman he love or commit the crime to save her and then lose her anyway. *Hot Fuzz*'s Nicholas Angel's discovery of the killers is accompanied by his lowest moment, in which he has to admit he can't solve the crime on his own and drive off into the darkness, leaving his new best friend behind. Writers do this to make their Crisis Points much more rich and complex.

As you create your own stories, you are free to combine these forms of Crisis Points in any way you want, as long as you keep one thing in mind: these are Points of No Return for the protagonist.

As mentioned above, once the protagonist encounters this Crisis Point, whether it is new information, a difficult decision, or an emotional peak, there is no turning back for them. They are on a high-speed trajectory towards the climax of their narrative. They are coming to the end of their story, and it is time for them to win or to lose.

This means the last portion of your story, that chunk between the Crisis Point and the Climax, needs to show your protagonist fighting harder than they have ever fought before. This is where the pacifist will commit murder. The doormat character will stand up for himself. The whisperer will learn to shout. In this period, the protagonist will break out of his or her shell or learn how to keep their mouth shut. It's where students will stand on desks shouting "Oh Captain, my Captain." It's where a hobbit will get his finger bitten off. An untitled woman will talk back to a Lady. This is the last battle with the "big boss" before winning the video game. This is the time when the character is ready to create a Climax.

Crafting Your Crisis Point

Write a paragraph about your protagonist's Crisis Point. As you write, consider the following tips:

1. As mentioned above, a Crisis Point can change based on what kind of story you are writing. What kind of Crisis Point do you plan on using? Now ask the hard question: why? Why is it important for you to use that specific kind of Crisis Point and not another option? Make sure you make the best choice for your story and not just choose something "just because."

2. A Crisis Point is a Point of No Return for your protagonist. How is your Crisis Point a major turning point for your character?

How can the protagonist never go back to who he or she was at the beginning of the story after crossing this point?

3. Students mistake a Crisis Point for just another obstacle. Have you picked the best moment for your Point of No Return? If you remove that scene/obstacle, will your story still work? If it will still work, then you haven't identified your Crisis Point correctly.

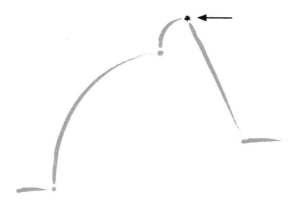

Chapter 9
Climax

By this point in the narrative, your protagonist will have experienced a lot. His or her world has been established and then thrown off kilter. He or she has set eyes on a goal and then fought like hell to win it. He or she has come up with multiple ways of succeeding, but is then knocked backwards by obstacle after obstacle. Finally, he or she hits that Point of No Return where an emotional peak, a difficult decision or new information shoves him or her towards a last major obstacle.

If a writer wants to end his or her story with a "happy" ending, then we will see the protagonist use all the skills he learned or the items he collected over the course of the story to overcome that final obstacle and win his goal. In *Wreck-It Ralph*, Ralph has learned how to accept himself for who he is, and, as a result, he's willing to die in order to save Vanellope and stop the cybugs from destroying Sugar Rush. He saves the world, helps Vanellope cross the race's finish line and proves himself a hero to the Nicelanders. In *Harry Potter and the Deathly Hallows*, Harry has learned the dangers of allowing others to step in and protect him. He leaves everyone behind, using the courage he gained from his earlier struggles to venture into the forest and let Voldemort kill him (thereby destroying one of the final horcruxes and leaving Voldemort vulnerable to death). Once resurrected, Harry uses all the magic he learned over the previous books to destroy He Who Must Not Be Named, saving both the magical and the ordinary worlds. These endings show how the character could only win their goal because of what they learned. It was impossible for them to win their goal when they first started their adventure. This makes the entire journey of the story feel important and relevant to the reader/viewer.

Often, when a writer wants to end the story without a happy ending, the character's biggest internal obstacle – also known as the character's tragic flaw – is the reason the protagonist is not able to overcome those last obstacles. In *King Lear*, it is Lear's obstinate pride that prevents him from realizing the gravity of his ordeal and leads to the death of his beloved daughter Cordelia. In *Breaking Bad*, Walter White wants desperately to protect his family, but it is also his pride preventing him from keeping his mouth shut and eventually leading to his family's ruin. In *Brokeback Mountain*, Ennis's inability to communicate keeps him isolated from everyone he loves, whether it is his wife, his lover or his daughter. Because of this flaw, he loses the love of his life. All of these "sad" endings result from the protagonist's inability to overcome their most pressing obstacle – themselves.

Ironically, however, a story can have a "sad ending" but the character can still win her or his goal. In the Tom Hanks film *Big*, Josh wins his goal of becoming a kid again, but he has to say good-bye to the woman he loves. In *Lord of the Rings*, Frodo saves the Shire but the psychological and physical wounds inflicted upon him on his journey are too much for him to bare, and so he chooses to symbolically die by taking the elven ships into the West. In *Harry Potter and the Order of the Phoenix*, Harry Potter wins his goal of discovering the source of his visions, but his beloved godfather gets murdered as a result. In *Se7en,* Detective Mills solves John Doe's riddle of serial killings, but it results in his own wife's beheading. These kinds of stories –where the idea of a "happy" or "sad" ending has nothing to do with whether or not they actually won their goal - are the primary reasons why we, as writers, need to isolate our emotions when looking at the next element of the Major Dramatic Curve: the Climax.

Emotional Versus Goal Climax

Most readers/viewers begin their love of stories and storytelling in a very passive fashion; as they read the text or watch the story on a screen or stage, they sit back and let it affect them. Instead of being more actively engaged in the story (analyzing it, dissecting it, breaking it down to study it's pieces), these early readers/viewers make their determination about the quality of a story based on how it affects them emotionally. Their most developed responses to a text will be something along the lines of "I loved it" or "I hated it."

These passive readers/viewers have come to understand the Climax as something very different from how the term is used in relationship to the Major Dramatic Curve. They understand a Climax as the big moment of emotional catharsis at the end of the narrative. This can be the grand moment where the guy sweeps in with a romantic gesture to win back the girl, or it could be when the evil monster finally meets his demise at the hands of the once innocent female protagonist. It's where Libby Day escapes the home of the women trying to kill her. It's when Harry Potter defeats Quirell/Voldemort. It's when boy gets girl or good conquers evil. For passive narrative consumers, this moment is the place they remember as the "end" of the movie.

This idea of an "Emotional Climax" is much different than the kind of Climax writers need to think about when writing their narratives. More active consumers of storytelling (which should include all writers who use the Major Dramatic Curve as part of their craft) understand the Climax to be the exact moment where the protagonist either wins or loses the goal. In some instances, the Emotional Climax and the MDC Climax can be the same moment, but usually this isn't the case. The Emotional Climax can happen before or after the Major Dramatic Curve Climax, depending on the story. The important thing to remember is that the Climax hasn't happened until the protagonist no longer needs to do anything to win the goal. It is 100% clear whether they have won or lost, and the story can end.

Let's take a look at how an Emotional Climax and a Major Dramatic Curve Climax operate differently in the film *The Fifth Element*. In this story, our protagonist is Korben Dallas, a former member of the Federated Army's Special Forces and current taxi driver. When we meet him in his Ordinary World, he is a down-on-his-luck cab driver. His inciting incident is the introduction of "Leeloo," a beautiful young woman who is much more than she seems. While the rest of the plot involves an attempt to save Mankind from an impending evil force, everything Korben does services his goal of trying to get the girl. The entire plot line of saving the world is secondary to his desire to win Leeloo's heart. When he tells her he loves her and a great beam of light shoots from her chest and destroys the Great Evil, this is the moment most passive viewers would consider the Climax. It's exciting, and the world is saved. But this isn't the end of Korben's goal. Yes, he was able to overcome his biggest internal flaw and admit he loves another person, but he hasn't won her just yet. Saving the world is the Emotional Climax, not the Major Dramatic Curve Climax. It's not until we see him in the recovery chamber, making love to Leeloo, before we know for a fact he won his goal. This is his Climax (pun intended). He got the girl, and now the film can end.

This example brings up a much broader topic of consideration. In most films, the A-plot of the protagonist trying to get his goal is rarely the first thing audiences remember when reflecting on a film. Usually, it's the much more emotional B-plot that sticks with them. Think of Romantic Comedies. This is a genre well-known for being "chick" stories because they usually revolve around two people falling in love. But have you ever noticed that the romance is actually the subplot and not the main plot? In *The Proposal*, Margaret's goal is to stay in the country. *You've Got Mail*'s A-plot is a businesswoman trying to save her small business from a corporate chain bookstore. *The 40-Year Old Virgin* is about a man befriending his co-workers and learning to accept himself. *Jerry Maguire* is an agent who has to save his career. None of these stories feature the romance as the A-plot (the protagonist's main goal in the story). In fact, the romance is usually an obstacle to the protagonist winning his or her goal. Margaret's growing feelings for Andrew make it hard for her to marry him to prevent deportation. *You've Got Mail*'s romantic leads are the owners of the conflicting bookstores. Andy's low self-esteem about his virginity lies in direct contrast to his new girlfriend's experienced expectations. The fact that Jerry Maguire's love interest is also his assistant makes for several bad choices in the name of his business. The romance is the obstacle, not the goal. But all of these narratives are usually remembered for the romantic elements.

Sometimes, it's because of this emotional memory that people think the Emotional Climax is actually the Major Dramatic Curve climax. If I asked ten people to identify the Climax of the wonderfully written romantic comedy *Romancing the Stone*, I would say nine of those people would pick the scene in which Jack appears outside Joan's NYC apartment with his newly purchased boat and his crocodile skin boots. This has to be the Climax right? I mean, the film is called *Romancing the Stone*. The Climax has to be when the romance solidifies. Even though it's the last scene of the film, and the film doesn't "feel" over until that scene, it's not the Climax in terms of the Major Dramatic Curve.

What is Joan's goal in this film? Does she want to find treasure and fall in love? That may be a need (emotional motivator) that drives some of her actions, but it isn't her primary goal. Remember we meet her in her Ordinary World as a romance writer. She lives in a tiny, New York City apartment with her cat, and it's very clear the worlds she creates for her romance novels are much more exciting than her real life. Her inciting incident comes when she arrives home to a trashed apartment, a terrified cat and a chilling phone call in which she is told her sister has been kidnapped and will be murdered if she doesn't bring a package she received in the mail to Colombia. Since the inciting incident is the external event that launches the protagonist after her goal, we can ask ourselves at this moment, what is her goal? She wants to save her sister. Everything she does for the rest of the film is because she wants to save her sister's life. Even when she agrees to find the hidden treasure with Jack, it's only because he tells her it will give her more leverage when trying to get her sister.

This means that Joan's A-plot is her pursuit to save her sister's life. Everything involving the romance with Jack is a subplot when you view this through the Major Dramatic Curve. Does it mean the relationship is less important? No, but it's not the main story, and that's really important for writers to remember when crafting their character's arc.

Now back to the question at hand: What is the Major Dramatic Curve Climax of *Romancing the Stone*? If her goal is to save her sister, then her Climax is when she wins her goal and saves her sister. That's when the story is over for Joan. Yes, we want to know if she and Jack will ever be reunited again, but that's the Falling action, not the Climax.

Whenever I work with beginning writers, this confusion over the Emotional Climax versus the Major Dramatic Curve Climax tends to be a big issue. Usually, one of the most helpful tips I give my new writers is to think of the Emotional Climax as the resolution of the B-plot. If the romance between Jack and Joan is the B-plot, then the Emotional Climax is seeing them together. In *The Fifth Element*, since the B-plot is saving the world, it makes sense the Emotional Climax is when Leeloo defeats the Great Evil. It makes the A-plot feel much more cold and uninteresting, but it's the protagonist's goal driving the story forward. If it wasn't for the protagonist making the decision to pursue whatever it is they want, then the rest of the story (those more emotionally engaging and interesting bits) wouldn't have happened. The key is to not forget about your A-plot climax.

Crafting Your Climax

Write out two paragraphs: one for your emotional climax and one for your Major Dramatic Curve (A-plot) climax. As you write, consider the following:

1. What is the A-plot of your narrative? In other words, what is the protagonist's main goal? Is your Major Dramatic Curve Climax the exact moment when your protagonist wins or loses that goal?

2. What is your B-plot? In other words, what is the underlying, emotional need your protagonist tries to fulfill through the story? Do they succeed or fail at the Emotional Climax? If not, why not?

3. Does your Climax answer your Major Dramatic Question with a clear "yes" or "no"? For example, the Major Dramatic Question of the Wizard of Oz is "Will Dorothy return home?" The Climax of the film is when Dorothy wakes up in Oz surrounded by her family. Therefore, the Major Dramatic

Question is answered with a clear "yes." What was the Major Dramatic Question you created for your narrative way back in Chapter Two? Can your Climax answer it with a yes or no? If not, why not?

4. Was the protagonist able to reach his or her goal because of the skills and knowledge acquired as a result of going through the journey of the narrative? Or, conversely, did your protagonist fail to reach his or her goal because of a lesson or skill the character failed to learn? If the protagonist wins too easily or loses because there was never a way they could win to begin with, the reader/viewer will feel cheated so make sure the ending feels like the character earned their win/loss. Is your Climax earned?

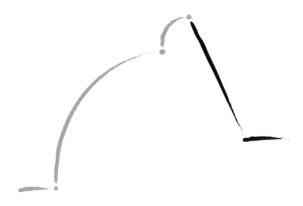

Chapter 10
The Rest is Silence

Once the protagonist has either won or lost the main goal of the A-plot, the story is basically over. After all, we are opening the book, turning on the TV, playing the game or watching the play because we want to see their journey towards their Climax. Why should we bother to stick around to see what happens after the story is basically over?

In many narratives, we don't. In *The Hunger Games*, Katniss wants to protect her sister. She wins her goal when she returns to District Twelve, an event that happens in the last chapter of the book. Yes, her internal dialogue gives us a sense that things aren't quite resolved, but for now, she's won her goal. The film adaptation does the same thing. Katniss arriving back home to her sister is the second to last shot of the film. We see one shot of President Snow looking menacing and biting his thumb, but other than that, the film is over.

Other narratives aren't able to wrap up so easily after the goal has been won. Sometimes, there are questions asked before the Climax that still need to be answered. In *Harry Potter and the Goblet of Fire*, Harry escapes Voldemort and his faithful servant, Barty Crouch Jr., but both Harry and the reader need to understand how Harry escaped. What happened when Harry and Voldemort's wands connected? Why did Wormtail take some of Harry's blood as part of Voldemort's resurrection? What happened to Alastor Moody? Will Barty Crouch Jr. still be a threat even though he has been captured? How will the Wizarding community, including the Minister of Magic react to the news of Voldemort's return? All of these questions need to be answered or at least hinted at in the last chapter of the book or else the reader will feel unsatisfied with their reading experience.

Using Falling Action

When a writer needs this extra time to wrap up any loose ends, the Major Dramatic Curve tells us it will be done in the period known as the Falling Action. This brief period of time between the Climax and the final moment of the story should be quite short. Remember, once the Climax has occurred, the story is over. We need to wrap it up and get out or the reader/viewer will lose patience with the story.

A great example of this can be seen in the final film version of *The Lord of the Rings: The Return of the King*. When I first saw this film in theaters, as soon as Frodo destroyed the Ring and the Tower of Barad-dûr (Sauron's Tower) fell, audience members began to get up out of their seats and head for the door. For them, the film was over, so it was time to run to the bathroom and get to their cars before the rush of the crowds leaving the theater. But there was still another 45 minutes of film left to go! Frodo and Sam needed to be saved by the Eagles and returned to Rivendell for care. Aragorn needed to accept his place as king of the humans and be reunited with his beloved Arwen. The Hobbits still needed to return to the

Shire where Sam marries Rosie Cotton and Frodo writes his book *There and Back Again*. Not to mention the fact that Frodo still needed to give up on a life in the Shire and journey into the West with the Elves and Bilbo. There was a *lot* more movie after the Ring was destroyed.

The reason why the film felt like it "ended multiple times" was because of the multitude of Major Dramatic Curves operating within that film series. Each film had it's own Curve, but there were also smaller, mini-Curves for Frodo, Aragorn and Sam. When the Ring was destroyed, this ended Sam's primary goal (protecting Frodo) which began at the end of Fellowship of the Ring. When Aragorn became King, it ended Aragorn's goal (protecting Mankind), which began in *The Two Towers*. Then, when Frodo admitted defeat and said the Shire hadn't been saved for him, it ended his goal (protecting the Shire). Frodo's goal begins the film series and ends the film series, but the conclusion of those smaller goals along the way made for a "never-ending" film viewing experience. While the writers of the screenplay, Peter Jackson, Fran Walsh and Philippa Boyens, understood what they were doing by closing the multiple Curves, the experience for many film watchers was a bit frustrating because they didn't know when the story would end.

To avoid this kind of "never-ending" feeling in our own work, it is important to keep the Falling Action to a minimum. In a perfect world, the Falling Action should be as short as possible – one chapter or less for a novel, three pages or less for a screenplay or stage play, one five minute cinematic or less for a game, etc. Answer any lingering questions and then end the story.

Keep in mind, however, that lingering questions can always be answered *before* the Climax of the film if the writer is crafty about it. In *The Goonies*, all the kids are reunited with their families. Steph and Mouth accept each other as friends. Chunk tells Sloth he will live with his family. The Fratellis are arrested, and Mikey throws away his inhaler. All of these are small events wrapping up unanswered questions. Mikey wins his goal of saving his neighborhood when the jewels are discovered in his marble bag – an event that takes place after all of the above mentioned falling action. His father rips up the contract, and the only thing left is for them to see the pirate ship sailing out into the ocean. By wrapping up the loose ends before the Climax, screenwriter Chris Columbus was able to end on the film as close to the Climax as possible, resulting in a tight and satisfying ending.

When it comes to Falling Action, a great rule of thumb to remember is this: When the goal is won, the story is done.

The New Place of Rest

Regardless of whether you have very little falling action or an entire chapter of it, there is one final stop on the protagonist's Curve, and that's his New Place of Rest. Also known as the Resolution, the New Place of Rest is where we get to see how much the character has changed (or not changed) as a result of the journey they have taken over the course of the story.

In many cases, the New Place of Rest is a mirror image of the first Resting Period. The hopelessly romantic, self-conscious hermit is now a worldly and confident woman in love. An orphan yearning for a real family has become a father and husband escorting his children on a traditional voyage to their new school. The under-appreciated and often ignored younger brother is now a leader looked up to by a large collection of his peers, including his big brother. An ostracized video game villain has proven his worth as another hero in his world. A victim of a serial killer has broken away from the label and taken charge of her own life and fate. Who these characters are at the end of their story is a direct result of leaving behind their Ordinary World to pursue a goal. During their adventure, they passed a Point of No Return (Crisis) that altered them forever.

It's important to include this Place of Rest for the same reason we want to focus on an active goal: readers and viewers of the stories we tell have signed on to the journey with our characters in order to vicariously travel on the adventure with our protagonist. Someone who feels weak or under-appreciated in their own lives may love super hero comics because it gives them the feeling of being powerful and useful. Someone unlucky in love might read a romance novel because they want to know what it feels like to be the object of someone's affection. Someone bored by the humdrum of their own life might watch a horror film to add excitement to their day. In order for them to really feel the impact of this journey, they need to know how the protagonist has changed as a result.

That's not to say that these changes need to be overly obvious. Katniss Everdeen starts off *The Hunger Games* as a strong female who serves as both mother and father to her younger sister. She hunts secretly in the woods and is able to trade on the black market because she is, in effect, invisible. At the end of both the book and the movie, we know she can never go back to being invisible again. Her days of operating in secrecy are over, and we are left questioning how this will affect the sister she loves and cares for. We are left knowing that she can't "forget" what happened as she hopes. She has seen people die. She has killed people. And now her attempt to save both herself and her fellow District member has backfired. She is on the Capitol's radar, and it might result in the death of everyone she loves. This new place of rest is subtle and mostly implied, especially in the film adaptation. But the change is evident.

Elizabeth Bennett's change is also rather subtle in *Pride and Prejudice*. While she is still the kind and proper girl she was at the beginning of the book, she has been humbled by the events of her journey. Once so quick to judge others, including her parents and the men in her town, she has been taught that her opinions of other people are not facts. She has learned to keep her silence in case she might not be quite correct in how she judges others.

Regardless of how subtle a transition the change might be, a writer must incorporate some kind of change to the protagonist. Otherwise, what was the point of a reader/viewer going on the adventure with them? What impact did the story have on the day-to-day dealings of the character's life? If the events of the story don't have any kind of impact, then why were those events important enough to write about them?

For writers who have a hard time figuring out how they want their protagonist to change, I recommend they think of lessons the journey might have taught the character. Even if a writer can't quite get their head around the idea of how their character has grown and changed, picking a concrete lesson for the character to learn can usually have the same effect. After all, a person must change every time they learn. In *The Goonies*, Mikey learns not to rely on others (symbolized by his inhaler) and to take charge of his own destiny. In *Wreck-It Ralph*, Ralph learns the lesson recited at the top of the film ("I'm bad, and that's okay"). In *Dark Places*, Libby Day learns she doesn't have to be a victim anymore. Elizabeth Bennett learns not to jump to conclusions about people based on first impressions. Dorothy learns there is no place like home.

The key thing to remember here is, just like the Falling Action, showing this New Place of Rest needs to take as little time as possible. Something as simple as a single action (throwing away an inhaler) or a single line of dialogue ("There's no place like home") can show this change. Spending too long on the change will have the same effect as spending too long on the Falling Action. Again, when the goal is won, the story is done.

But What About The Sequel?

A common question I get asked when it comes to the end of a story is this: What if this is just part one of a larger story? This is a valid question, especially since many publishers love to purchase a series over a stand-alone novel. This is because the audience gained by the first book will help feed the marketing of the second book and so on. So what do you do? Do you end the first book somewhere in the middle of the Rising Action?

Even if you are writing a novel series, it's always best for your first novel to be structured around a self-contained Major Dramatic Curve. Only the Falling Action should contain the obvious set-up for the next chapter in the larger story. A great example is *The Hunger Games*. The first book contains a complete narrative arc with hints at a possible sequel. Katniss is incited when her sister's name is called at the Reaping. Her goal is to save her sister, which includes volunteering for her and then returning home afterwards so she can take care of her sister. Her primary tactic – to try to win the Hunger Games. Her primary obstacles are the Hunger Games, the other tributes, and the traps set-up by the game-makers. She wins her goal when she returns to her sister, but during the Falling Action, we get the hint that not all is well in Katniss's world. If a reader chose to only read the first book, they would feel satisfied with their reading experience, even if they don't pick up *Catching Fire* or *Mockingjay*. This complete curve gave readers a full, satisfying story, while still opening up the world for future books in the same series.

Screenplays are not sold the same way books are, and should never be written with a sequel in mind. If a screenwriter is lucky enough to sell their original screenplay, they need to make sure it has a complete beginning, middle, and end. If the screenplay sells and the production company or studio is excited about the story, they can always request a rewrite of the film, allowing for an more open-ended structure, before the screenplay goes into production. The only exception to this would be if the project has been commissioned by a producer who has a guaranteed distribution deal for multiple pictures.

Crafting Your Falling Action and New Place of Rest

Write a paragraph about your protagonist's Falling Action and New Place of Rest. As you write, consider the following:

1. What unanswered questions do you need to answer after the character has won or lost the main goal (after the Climax)? Is there a way to answer these questions *before* the Climax? If not, why not?

2. If you have to have a Falling Action, how long will it take to complete that section? What remains to keep the reader/viewer engaged in the narrative? What will the story gain by including that section?

3. How does your protagonist's New Place of Rest compare to their initial Resting Period? How have they changed/morphed, transformed as a character? What lessons have they learned or failed to learn? How has she or he improved or declined as a human being? How can you SHOW these things? If they haven't changed, what is the significance of their narrative? Why would a reader/viewer bother going on the adventure with them to begin with?

4. Have you completed your narrative or opened it up for sequels? If you are planning on having sequels to your story, then do you have a complete Major Dramatic Curve in your first narrative? If not, why not? Is it possible to have a complete Curve that serves as the first chapter in a larger world?

5. What is the final line or image you will use to end your narrative? Just like the first impression is important, leaving the reader/viewer with a lasting final moment is key.

Part 3

Using the Character Arc

Good story' means something worth telling
that the world wants to hear.
Finding this is your lonely task...
But the love of a good story,
of terrific characters and a world
driven by your passion, courage,
and creative gifts is still not enough.
Your goal must be a good story well told.
— Robert McKee

Chapter 11
Using The Major Dramatic Curve: A Practical Guide

Now that you have studied each element of the Curve on its own and saw how those pieces worked together to form a complete and well developed Character Arc, there is still one question remaining: How do you practically apply what you've learned to your own writing?

The answer varies based on two major factors: 1) Where are you in your writing process and 2) in what format are you writing?

Within the Writing Process

Based on where you are within your writing process, how you use this Curve will vary slightly. As with any kind of craft technique, once you think about the Major Dramatic Curve in relation to your story, you may find yourself in need of drastic changes. This isn't anything to panic about. Just remember the writing process is a process, and rewriting will only get you closer and closer to your individual writing goal.

If you are still in the planning phases of your writing project, you will be happy to know this is the easiest time to apply the Major Dramatic Curve. Whether you develop your story by free writing, outlining, mind-mapping or any other method, you should be able to incorporate the ideas of this book without too much stress. Simply ask yourself what elements of the Curve already exist in your planned story:

Do you establish your protagonist in their Ordinary World?

Do you have some kind of external event that launches your protagonist after a goal?

Is your protagonist an active or reactive character?

What is the goal?

What are the tactics your character uses to try to win that goal?

What stands in his or her way (obstacles)?

What is a Point of No Return (Crisis Point) moment that occurs near the end of the story?

What is the Climax of the story?

Is it the moment where the protagonist wins the goal or have you identified an Emotional Climax by mistake?

What lingering questions need to be tied up before the end of the story?

Can you tie them up before the Climax to reduce the amount of time spent on Falling Action?

What is the New Place of Rest for your protagonist?

How does it mirror the way in which we first met him or her?

What lessons did your character learn as a result of this struggle?

For plotters, this should be a very fun and invigorating process of question and answer. Plotters are writers who plan ahead. The way they discover their world is through outlining, building character bibles or other preparation based methods of idea development. These are the writers who usually know every event of their story (or very nearly every event) before they sit down to write a word.

Purgers, however, might find this kind of questioning a bit more frustrating. Purgers are the writers who discover their story by writing it. These are the writers who spend years developing a narrative because they aren't entirely sure where they want it go before they begin. They discover the characters, the world and the plot by rewriting it, again and again, often throwing out hundreds, if not thousands, of pages of writing in the process. For these kinds of writers, they may find themselves saying "I don't' know!" to many of the questions pertaining to the Major Dramatic Curve: "What's your Climax?" Um... I don't know. "What's your protagonist's goal?" I don't know. "Who is your protagonist?" I don't know!

There has long been the debate as to which kind of writers are best: Plotters or Purgers. Plotters tend to be more adept at creating faster-paced stories with a solid structure but their characters and world building are often lacking. Conversely, Purgers tend to better world and character builders, but their plots lack structure and they tend to take much longer to complete a project. In my opinion, there is plenty of room in the world for both kinds of writers, but it's usually a good idea to try to find a middle ground when it comes to applying the Major Dramatic Curve.

My recommendation to anyone in the beginning stages of writing a story is to use a synopsis (also known as a treatment or golden path play-through) to develop the Major Dramatic Curve. Even if you aren't completely sure where your story will end up, write the synopsis of your story in its entirety. Purgers, as you write, those holes in your story will begin to fill in. Plotters, as you write, you will see the bigger picture of your final story. This synopsis shouldn't be short, but don't feel like you have to include every detail. You aren't writing the completed book or script. You are writing a synopsis. A good rule of thumb is to try to use one page of treatment for every 25 pages of script or one page of summary for every 8500 words planned. Obviously, you never completely know how long your final story will wind up, but use broad generalities based on the format or genre in which you write. Screenplays tend to be about 110 pages. Young Adult novels tend to be about 60,000 words. Mainstream, adult novels are about 85,000 words. Fantasy/sci-fi novels can be anywhere from 85,000 to 150,000 words. Use your best guesses and do your research to find the market length is of similar stories in your genre.

Once you have completed your synopsis or treatment, print it out and grab a highlighter (or use a highlighting feature on your word processing software) and look for the major elements of the Major Dramatic Curve. Identify the Place of Rest, Inciting Incident, Tactics and Obstacles of the Rising Action, Crisis Point and Climax. How much Falling Action do you have before you establish the New Place of Rest?

When you are done, you can look at your highlighted areas and assess what elements need to be addressed in order to have a fully developed Major Dramatic Curve. You might be missing a Crisis Point, or you might have way too much Place of Rest before your Inciting Incident. Once you know what you need to do, you can put that synopsis aside and write a brand new one that addresses the changes you decided to make. Continue to highlight and re-write until your synopsis is as perfect as you can make it. Then you can break the synopsis apart, picking what story elements will go into which chapters or acts and use it as a living outline of your narrative.

If you have already written a part or all of your story, then you will want to stop where you are and write up a synopsis as well. Include everything in that synopsis, including the sections of the story you have already written. This will force you to rethink what you wrote and honestly assess if you have too much backstory or not enough time before your Inciting Incident.

Stories tend to fall apart in two places: the very beginning or the middle. Unfortunately, we can sometimes be so close to our stories we become blind to its faults. I've also seen many beginning writers who think of what they have already written as being written in stone: "I already wrote it, so I can't change it!" This is why it's so important to step away from what you have already written and write it fresh in a synopsis. Writing it again in a new document will often help you see what you might have been blind to before. You may have too much world building (Place of Rest) before your story starts. Or you might not have established your character's personality before the Inciting Incident. If you are too close to your story because you have already taken the time and creative energy to write some of it, then stepping away and looking at it with fresh eyes may be the most important thing you ever do for your writing career.

Once you have written and highlighted your synopsis, you have two choices: 1) get right into rewriting your story or 2) you can continue to re-write your synopsis, again and again, highlighting and making changes, until you know exactly how you want your final story to build. I highly recommend going with option two because of the reduced workload it creates in the long run. Rewriting a six-page synopsis will take a lot less time than rewriting 51000 words or 70 pages of a screenplay. However, some writers don't work that way. They get so excited about the changes they want to make, they dive right in and make those changes without looking at the bigger picture. Both ways can be effective, but it might take a lot more time if you don't take the time to rewrite your synopsis.

What Are You Writing

The wonderful thing about the Major Dramatic Curve is that it works across writing formats. The concepts here can be used in novels, short stories, web series, comic books, screenplays, stage plays, graphic novels, games, television shows and other narrative formats we have yet to develop. The flexibility of this structure exists because of the universal nature of its primary component – a protagonist with an active goal.

How we apply this flexible structure to various formats takes a bit of thought and adaptation. We know each story, regardless of format, needs a Place of Rest at the beginning of the story, but how much is enough? We know the Crisis Point needs to come near the end of the story, but where exactly at the end? How close to or far away from the Climax should it be? Let's look at each of these elements in turn:

The Place of Rest leading to the Inciting Incident – In the world of screenwriting, this element is rather cut and dry. As I explained in Chapter One, screenwriters are told their Inciting Incident must come on page 10 or page 12 (depending on whether the writer follows Field's or Snyder's guidelines). Therefore, those first 9-11 pages leading up to the Inciting Incident will be the Place of Rest.

In the world of novel writing, there is much more flexibility in the length of the Place of Rest and the placement of the Inciting Incident. Young Adult novels tend to have the first chapter serve as the Place of Rest with the Inciting Incident occurring at the end of the first chapter. *The Hunger Games*, Chapter One, ends with Prim's name being called at the Reaping. Many other shorter (45,000-75,000) novels do the same thing in the interest of getting to the main storyline faster. The exception is when Chapter One is meant to take the place of a Prologue in terms of world building (Prologues tend not to be used as much in writing the way they once were. One explanation for this is modern readers tend to skip over prologues and epilogues because they don't feel/know they are part of the story. Authors counter this by simply marking their prologues/epilogues as chapters). For example, in *Harry Potter and The Sorcerer's/Philosopher's Stone*, Chapter One shows Harry being left at his aunt and uncle's home as a baby. This would have been called a Prologue in another era.

Longer books, especially fantasies, however, may take a bit longer to get to the Inciting Incident. Because the book has more of a breadth to its length, the reader knows he/she has signed on to a longer story. Fantasy stories might use those extra pages for world building. Epic romances may do the same thing in order to establish customs or rituals. Some stories might use this extra space to wrap up a past saga while setting up the new one. *The Lord of the Rings: The Fellowship of the Ring* (1954) does this nicely. The beginning of the book wraps up the plotline of Bilbo Baggins, first introduced in his own book, *The Hobbit*, in 1937. Tolkien wanted readers to know what happened to this beloved figure and then pass the torch onto the new protagonist, Frodo Baggins, several chapters later.

It's important to remember, however, that we are not J.R.R. Tolkien, and so we want to get to the heart of our story as soon as we can. Remember, we live in an era where readers are used to plot based narratives (mostly because of the rise in popularity of films, TV shows and games), and so we want to limit that world building material to only what is truly essential. If you can introduce some world building after the Inciting Incident, then try to do that as much as you can.

A good general guideline would be to try to introduce your Inciting Incident no more than 1/12 of the way into your story. This holds true across the format-board. If you are writing a television pilot that is 50 pages long (60 minutes with commercials), that means your inciting incident should happen on or around page 5 (Halfway through Act One if you don't have a teaser). If you are writing a graphic novel that will wind up 180 pages long, then shoot for an Inciting Incident happening on page 15. For a serialized comic book, the end of your first issue is a great place to use your Inciting Incident as a cliffhanger, as long as your Place of Rest is engaging enough to form the heart of the first issue.

In a short story, you have a lot less space so choose your Inciting Incident and Place of Rest wisely. Remember we need to know who the protagonist was before their world was thrown off balance, but with so little room, this might mean you telling us after they have been Incited what has changed. This form of flashing back to the Place of Rest is similar to what many game writers do (see Chapter Five). Just as character traits, equipment slots and descriptors can tell us about a character's past in a game, details about the characters, their actions and lines of dialogue can give us a sense of who they were in a short story.

Rising Action – Regardless of what kind of format you write, it's important to remember the bulk of your story needs to exist in this section. Ask yourself the following questions: What are all the tactics my protagonist uses to win her or his goal? What stands in his or her way? Is my protagonist fighting for this goal like her or his life depends on it? What's at stake? What will he or she lose if the goal isn't won? How can I increase the stakes? What can I do to my character to make it seem like she or he couldn't possibly win? What are the obstacles standing in my character's way? How can I make these obstacles harder to overcome?

Remember, a protagonist can't just sit back and react to everything. She or he needs to be actively fighting for the goal. It should feel like the protagonist's life will change forever if she or he doesn't win. There has to be something important wrapped up in this journey for the protagonist or else the cathartic experience the reader/viewer wants to have as a result of sharing this narrative will be decreased.

I have one warning for novel and short story writers getting ready to tackle their Rising Action. Anyone working in prose has a distinct advantage over other types of writers: we are allowed to look inside a character's head. This means you can use a character's low self-esteem, doubts or fear as some of their obstacles. It's important, however, you don't restrict your obstacles to these internal factors. For a protagonist to actively fight for a goal, we need to "see" them doing something. We want to see Bella jumping off mountains and driving dangerous motorcycles, not

Bella reacting to someone staring at her for an entire book. Make your protagonist active, and don't fall prey to a beginner's mistake of making the majority of the obstacles internal. Internal obstacles lead to a passive protagonist instead of an active protagonist. As mentioned in Chapter Two, there are successful reactive protagonists out there, but it's always best to challenge yourself to write active main characters whenever you can.

Crisis Point – The Crisis Point, as a general rule, usually happens about 3/4 of the way through any given narrative. For screenwriters, this means it usually happens right around the Plot Point Two. It can happen just before it, just after it, or the Crisis Point and Plot Point Two can be the same event. It all depends on the components of your individual story. If you use the *Save the Cat* Beat sheet, your Crisis Point is the same thing as your All is Lost moment, occurring on page 75.

For all other writers, you can just use the 3/4 guideline to help you out. If you are writing an 80,000 word novel, then you safely place your Crisis Point right around your 60,000 word mark. For TV Writers, your four act structure makes it easy to find a Crisis Point at the end of Act Three. If you are writing a comic series, it's really going to come down to how many issues you are planning and how many pages each issue lasts. But if you have a twelve issue series, then ending your 8th issue with a Crisis Point would be a great cliffhanger for your readers.

Trying to put your Crisis Point earlier than the 3/4 mark results in the pacing of the story dragging a bit between the Crisis Point and the Climax. Once we have that earth-shattering Point of No Return, we know the character has fundamentally changed. We want to see the consequences of that change, for good or for bad.

The Climax, Falling Action and New Place of Rest – As mentioned several times, when the goal is won, the story is done. The same is true if the goal is lost. Remember the protagonist's goal is what drives the main story, so once that goal is resolved (won or lost), there's really no reason to stick around. In films, you will often see the Emotional Climax occur between 5-10 minutes before the end of the film, but the Major Dramatic Curve climax can occur as late as the last page or scene. Sometimes this is reversed (as with *Romancing the Stone* where the Emotional Climax occurs after the Major Dramatic Curve Climax), but as a general rule, both Climaxes should occur within the last five minutes of the film.

With novels, it's important to get to the Climax as close to the end as possible, but there is a bit more flexibility. As I mentioned before, there is an entire chapter in *Harry Potter and the Goblet of Fire* after Harry's escape from Barty Crouch Jr. and this is seen in other places in the series as well. JK Rowling gives us a satisfying Climax but then uses one additional chapter to wrap things up, usually ending with Harry getting onto the Hogwarts Express or otherwise preparing for his trip back to the Dursley's home. The key to remember is that the story is complete once the goal has been won or lost, so tying up those loose ends and ending the story is extremely important. If the reader feels like the story is done, there is nothing to stop them from putting down the book, especially if it feels like it drags on.

In other formats, the same underlying truth holds: end the play, the comic, the web series, etc. You're player has destroyed the Big Boss, so end the game. When the goal is won, the story is done.

Guidelines More Than Actual Rules

Regardless of where you are in the writing process, the most important thing to remember is not to lose heart. You are learning the material in this book, but if your story doesn't quite fit into the mold of what I'm suggesting here, it doesn't mean your story is "bad." Creativity takes on many forms, and the materials here are meant to act as guidelines and not hard and fast rules.

Chapter 12
The Exceptions to the Rule

New forms of storytelling have emerged, and those new forms don't always follow the same underlying structures as its predecessors. In this chapter, I'm going to look at a few variations on the traditional narrative structure and look at how the Major Dramatic Curve can adapt to each of them.

Multiple Protagonists

While the traditional Major Dramatic Curve focuses on just one main character, more and more narratives are popping up where you can't quite identify one, solitary lead. Sometimes a story isn't about just one person, and those kinds of stories deserve just as much attention to character development as all the rest.

When it comes to writing a multiple protagonist narrative, first a writer needs to honestly ask what the dramatic function of each main character truly is. Sometimes, you might think you have multiple protagonist when really, you don't. *Bill & Ted's Excellent Adventure* is a great "buddy" film where a viewer might believe, at first glance, that two protagonist's drive this storyline. But if you really analyze the story, you will notice that Ted (Keanu Reeves) really drives the action. They both need to pass history, but Ted has the most to lose. If they don't pass, he will be shipped off to Alaska. It's also Ted who makes most of the plot choices that really drive the story, including going to talk to the princess in Medieval England and going back in time to steal his father's keys. Bill might have just as much screen time as Ted, but this doesn't automatically grant him a place as co-protagonist. If you are writing a narrative similar to *Bill & Ted*, then you want to make sure you really have multiple protagonists and not just multiple leading characters – there is a difference!

Some narratives, however, really are ensemble pieces. You can have multiple stories that only intersect in minor places, such as Amy Tan's *The Joy Luck Club* or the Richard Curtis film *Love Actually*, or you can have narratives where the lives of the characters intersect throughout the narrative, such as the television show *Downton Abbey*. The important thing to remember with these kinds of stories is that each character needs to have a unique and fully developed Major Dramatic Curve. How you make those Curves interact is part of the creative process that makes your story unique. Let's look at how the three above named narratives operate:

In *The Joy Luck Club*, Amy Tan explores how well four first generation Chinese American women know their mothers and how their perspective on life in America varies from their mothers' more traditional views. Amy Tan has eight characters to explore – the four mothers and the four daughters. Each character receives her own chapter (or chapters) in which to tell their story. The chapters are unique and each has the ability to stand alone. Together, this collection of short stories points to a larger picture of the first generation Chinese American culture. Since each chapter stands alone, it's no surprise that each chapter also contains its own, unique Major Dramatic Curve. Each chapter has a beginning-middle-end driven by a singular goal. Lindo fights to honor her parents even after being matched to the worst husband possible. Jing-mei fights to live up to her mother's dream of her becoming a prodigy. Ying-ying fights to motivate her daughter to bring out her "inner tiger" and treat herself well. Each woman has an active Curve with all the elements in place: Place of Rest, Inciting Incident, Rising Action, Crisis Point, Climax and Falling Action/New Place of Rest. (*The Joy Luck Club* offers great examples of how to apply the Dramatic Curve within the limited space of short stories.)

Like *The Joy Luck Club*, the film *Love Actually* also creates a larger picture by presenting us with a number of short stories featuring interconnected characters. While film has the ability to give us each story as a complete unit (see the film *Four Rooms* for a great example of this), *Love Actually* intertwines each Major Dramatic Curve so we see each Curve develop together. When the film opens, we meet each of the major characters of the film in their Place of Rest: aging rock star Billy Mack records a single he knows is terrible, dotting Jamie leaves his sick girlfriend to go to a wedding, mourning Daniel calls his best friend to talk about his recently deceased wife, a new Prime Minister walks into Downing Street for the first time. As the audience gets introduced to each character, we immediately get a sense of what kind of person they are.

Almost right away, we see each plotline's Inciting Incident: Billy Mack hears a radio DJ saying his new album is terrible, and he decides to use this to his advantage. Daniel finds out his stepson is in love for the first time and uses this as a bonding opportunity after his wife's death. Jamie meets his new non-English speaking maid, Aurelia, and tries to find a way to communicate with her. The new Prime Minister falls for his catering manager, Natalie ("That is so inconvenient") and must battle his emotions while trying to run the entire country. We bounce from storyline to storyline, staying relatively consistent in terms of where we are on the Major Dramatic Curve. The Crisis Points come together, and the Climaxes come together. This makes the overall film feel like a cohesive unit, working together to tell a great story.

In this case, you could almost unite the various plotlines under a conceptual protagonist – Love. At the beginning of the film, Love's Place of Rest is that it has been beaten down in some way, shape or form: a professional career that's lost its excitement, a girlfriend who has cheated, an unrequited love who has married your best friend, a career man who never had time for love. Then, we see a spark that gives Love a chance to succeed (see the Inciting Incidents listed above). The rest of the film shows Love trying to answer the dramatic question, Will Love conquer all? Each plotline explores a different kind of love to see if it can beat the odds and win out in the end. To help unite all aspects of the film, the movie both opens and closes with the idea of love at an airport – a physical symbol of the idea of love being a universal theme.

The Paul Haggis film *Crash* follows a similar multiple storyline, theme-driven structure as well. In this narrative, we look at the battle between racism and tolerance in a similar fashion. From a conceptual point of view, we can look at the Major Dramatic Question of this film as Will Tolerance defeat Racism? In each plotline, we see how racism emerges in every day life and how the multiracial characters deal with it.

Unlike *Love Actually*, the individual narratives in *Crash* aren't quite so in sync when it comes to introducing us to each character's Major Dramatic Curve. As we experience each story, we see each Curve develop at various places in the film. For example, we first see Jean and Rick's Curve when they are mugged in Santa Monica. The locksmith who comes to their house to change their locks, Daniel, experiences some racism at their house, but his Curve doesn't really begin until we see his interaction with the shopkeeper, Farhad. All of the Major Dramatic Curve elements are present for each character, but they are sprinkled in over time instead of being presented together.

Some narratives can take this wide distribution of Major Dramatic Curve elements a step further. Stories like *Downton Abbey*, that don't unite all their storylines with a theme or concept, can have even greater flexibility in how they present their Major Dramatic Curve elements. In Season One, the main conflict of the show involves the question of what will happen to Downton Abbey now that the heir has died on the Titanic. Once Robert, the Earl of Grantham, decides to pass the estate over to Matthew Crawley, a distant cousin who works for a living and is not used to living life in the family's traditional fashion, the show's twists and turns all involve Matthew's attempts to adapt to his new life as the future Earl of Grantham.

While the pilot (first) episode of the show is driven by Robert's goal of protecting the estate, the rest of the show features multiple characters, both servants and ladies and gentlemen of the house, fighting for what they want. Mary Crawley fights to find a good husband. Matthew's mother Violet fights to correct the Crawley family's "outdated" way of life. Servant Gwen fights to improve her position in life by learning to type and then applying for jobs as a secretary. Cook Mrs. Padmore fights to keep her job despite evolving technologies and failing eyesight. Lady Sybil fights to claim her role as a liberated woman, and footman Thomas just tries to screw up as much as he can for his personal amusement. With each character, we see their goals introduced and paid off in various episodes. Many times, we will see a new Curve introduced just as another one is paid off. This keeps the viewer engaged in the show throughout the season and prevents the show from ever feeling like it is dragging.

Each of these multi-protagonist stories are all exceedingly different in terms of structure, plot and themes but they all have the same thing in common: fully developed Major Dramatic Curves for any and all major characters.

The Storyteller Structure

Sometimes, a narrative is told through the eyes of another individual or individuals. In other words, one character in the story relates another character's tale in order to drive the narrative forward. I call this kind of narrative structure The Storyteller Structure. In this type of story, the storyteller has a very clear goal, and he or she uses the story as a tactic to win that goal.

A great example of this kind of structure is the film version of *The Princess Bride*. The story revolves around a grandfather reads a book to his sick grandson. The story of the book is the love story between Westley and Buttercup, two soul mates separated by class, monsters and even death. If you asked a passive viewer who the protagonist of this film would be, that viewer might immediately choose Buttercup or Westley since they are the "main" characters of the story within the story. But remember a protagonist is the character whose goal drives the story forward, and while both of these characters are interesting, you can't really say one or the other one really drives the plot. The real protagonist of the film is the Grandfather (Peter Falk). He has a very clear goal, and he tells the story of Westley and Buttercup in order to win that goal.

What is the Grandfather's goal, you may ask? Think about the opening of the film: the Grandson is sick, and his Grandfather comes over to read him a story. The Grandson would prefer to lie in bed and play video games, but the Grandfather has other plans. "It was the book my father use to read to me when I was sick, and I used to read it to your father, and today, I'm gonna read it to you." While we aren't entirely sure where the sick Grandson's father currently is, we get the idea he might be deceased. Therefore, the Grandfather's goal is to reignite a tradition that means a lot to him. He wants his Grandson to continue the legacy of reading to their sons when they are sick. This is why the Grandfather happily skips some sections of the book ("They're kissing again...") in order to keep the Grandson engaged. He wants to keep him interested in the tradition. We know the Grandfather wins his goal at the end of the story because the Grandson says "Maybe you can come and read it to me again." The story of Westley and Buttercup is the most interesting story, but it's the B-plot from a structural point of view. The A-plot is the storyteller Grandfather fighting to reestablish a family tradition.

If you are familiar with the novel version of The Princess Bride, the storyteller structure is also present in that text. While the Grandfather and Grandson of the film are absent, a father is "editing" the story of Westley and Buttercup into a "good parts version" for his son. The father's goal is to make the story acceptable to his son in order to reclaim what he once shared with his own father.

Another great example of the Storyteller Structure is *The Notebook*, written by Nicholas Sparks and then adapted to the screen by Jeremy Leven. In this story, a man (named Duke in the film but Noah in the book) reads a story of young love to a woman suffering from Alzheimer's. As he tells her the story, it becomes clear the female lead of the story is a younger version of the woman listening. The reader is an older version of Noah, the young man in the story, and his active goal is to get his wife to remember who he is. By reading their story (written by Noah in the book and Allie in the movie), Old Noah fights to get his beloved wife back, even if just for a moment. Once again, the A-plot is the Storyteller, and so this is where the elements of the Major Dramatic Curve can be seen. The story is just a primary tactic and not the main story.

Other examples of the Storyteller structure are *The Great Gatsby* and *Slumdog Millionaire*, but there are slightly varied versions of this structure as well. One variation of the Storyteller structure can be seen when a character gathers the story from another source instead of telling the story to others. This is most often scene when some kind of interviewer – usually a detective, reporter, lawyer or judge – tries to gather information from a number of sources. In *The Cuckoo's Calling*, private detective Cormoran Strike tries to piece together how a famous celebrity was murdered by interviewing a number of people who knew her. As he gathers evidence, we get to experience Lula Landry's story. We get to know her as Cormoran fights to win his goal of solving the case. *Interview with The Vampire* similarly tells us the memorable story of Louis, Lestat and Claudia via an interviewer. The interviewer wants to convince Louis to make him a vampire, and the primary way he tries to accomplish this is by getting Louis to tell his story. Louis uses his story to try to convince the interviewer that he doesn't want to be a vampire, but it fails. In the film version of *The Sweet Hereafter*, lawyer Mitchell Stephens questions the various witnesses of the school bus accident. As he hears their stories, so do we. Similarly, the majority of *Citizen Kane* is also told via interviews with people who know Kane throughout his life. In all of these examples, it is the person gathering the details of the story who drives the story forward. This means the interviewer is the protagonist, and the main story we remember after reading or viewing the tale is the B-plot. Other examples of this variation of the Storyteller Structure include *Velvet Goldmine*, *Big Fish*, and *The Silkworm*.

A much more subtle use of the Storyteller Structure can be seen in the Ian McEwen novel and Christopher Hampton screenplay adaptation of *Atonement*. In both versions of the story, the reader/viewer can't quite choose the protagonist of the story until the very end of the narrative. While there are clues (change in novel structure in the book and the ongoing sound effect of the typewriter in the movie), it's not entirely clear that Briony is the protagonist until she tells us she has manipulated all we have seen until this point. Briony's goal is to find atonement for the false accusation she made as a child that ultimately lead to the death of Robbie, a young servant educated by her father and in love with her sister. The primary tactic Briony uses to gain her atonement is by changing the events of the story. She manipulates what we know about the characters so she can give them the happy ending she stole from them. She is the most unreliable of narrators, but every change she makes serves her goal of fighting for forgiveness. At the end of the story, the storyteller's goal is clear and going back and re-reading the book or re-watching the film shows you who how were manipulated in a brilliant and structurally sound way.

Keep in mind that having a storyteller doesn't automatically mean the Storyteller Structure is being used. The film *Edward Scissorhands* opens with an older version of Kim telling her granddaughter about Edward in order to explain why it snows. While this seems like a great set-up for a storyteller structure, the film never returns to the older version of Kim, and therefore doesn't pay off the structure as a whole. In fact, that opening scene could be completely cut from the film, and it wouldn't affect the overall viewing experience at all.

Similarly, the film *Moulin Rouge!* is framed by Christian writing the story of his and Satine's love affair. While this appearance of our storyteller is much more consistent throughout the film (we cut back to him quite often to see his reaction to the events of the story), the film could have worked just as well without him. Christian and Satine have very clear and active goals that don't need the storyteller's involvement to succeed or fail. While the addition of the storyteller may have helped with pacing and delivery of the story, the main plot is still the love affair.

For a Storyteller Structure to work, the Storyteller needs to have an active goal, and the story he or she tells has to be a tactic the Storyteller uses in order to win that goal. In other words, the story wouldn't exist if not for the presence of the storyteller. If you are writing this kind of narrative – where the story is a byproduct of the storyteller's journey – then make sure all elements of the Major Dramatic Curve exist on the storyteller's narrative Curve since this is the driving factor behind the story as a whole.

Flashback/Flash-forward

Non-linear storytelling is a regular part of our modern day cultural narrative structures. Whether we merely have a flashback or we completely shake up the chronology of a story, manipulating time has become a well-known and useful tool we can use to tell unique and compelling stories. The key to making sure these kinds of stories work is to make sure that two things are true: 1) there is a reason to manipulate time and 2) all elements of the Major Dramatic Curve are still in place.

Let's first look at a narrative that manipulated time in a way that didn't work: the film *21 Grams*. With a compelling story and a dynamic cast, this film had every reason to be an emotional powerhouse. The story focuses on how a freak accident impacts the lives of three people: the woman who lost her husband and daughter, the man who hit them, and the man who received a heart transplant from the dead husband. If all the pieces were told in a chronological fashion, there is a clear and compelling Curve driving the story forward in a dynamic way. But the director and editor made the decision to tell this story in a nonlinear fashion. The choice resulted in a rather frustrating watch for the viewer. While the stunning performances received high praise, critics called the film "frustratingly flawed" and referred to the structure as a "parlor game" that "doesn't let any of the characters build an arc of growth or despair." The filmmakers may have chosen to tell the story in a nonlinear fashion because they thought it would be "cool" or "interesting," but the problem was that the story didn't provide the motivation for a nonlinear tale.

If you are considering using a nonlinear structure to tell your story, remember form follows function. The story should contain elements that warrant the use of a non-traditional story structure in order for it to work. These elements can be character-driven or thematic in nature, but they need to exist.

Two great narratives that use character as justification for nonlinear storytelling are *The Time Traveler's Wife* by Audrey Niffenegger and the Christopher Nolan film *Memento*. In both narratives, the protagonist suffers from a medical condition that causes them to see the world in a non-traditional way. This, in turn, justifies the story being delivered to us in a non-traditional way as well. In *The Time Traveler's Wife*, protagonist Henry DeTamble has Chrono-Impairment, a disease that causes him to involuntarily travel back and forth in time. As he experiences his life "out of order," we experience his story out of order. The chronology matches his point of view, and so the structure works.

Similarly, *Memento's* Leonard was shot in the head and, as a result, he can't form any new memories. He has to remind himself where he is and what he's doing by writing himself notes or tattooing information to his skin. His short-term memory loss results in his experiencing the world around him in bursts. In order to allow us to experience the world in the same fashion, Christopher Nolan presents Leonard's story in a "pendulum" fashion. We start at one extreme of his time line (the far future), then swing back and see the other extreme of his time line (the distant past). We cut back and forth – one narrative moving forward and another moving backward – until we meet in the middle of his timeline. This cutting back and forth mimics the way Leonard receives information in bursts. As he must piece together what's happening in his world, so must we, the viewers. This works because we are placed in his shoes and forced to see the world in the same way he sees it.

With both of these stories, what's fascinating is that even though we experience their story out of order, we are still presented with their Major Dramatic Curves in a linear fashion. In *The Time Traveler's Wife*, we experience Henry's relationship with Claire as a fully developed, linear Major Dramatic Curve. We see their meeting, growing fondness for each other, marriage, pregnancy and death all in the right order. Similarly, in *Memento*, we see Leonard's journey towards avenging his wife's murder in a fully developed Curve – in fact, two of them! Both his forward progressing story and his backward progressing story have completely developed Major Dramatic Curves. Because the Curves are presented in a traditional order, the nonlinear narrative works.

Nonlinear narratives using conceptual or thematic protagonists can also work as long as the Major Dramatic Curve travels in a linear fashion as well. The most famous example of this can be seen with Quentin Tarantino's *Pulp Fiction*. In this story, the film begins and ends in the middle of a timeline – a scene in a diner. The film cuts backwards and forwards, circling back and forth in time. With seemingly no rhyme or reason about where we will go next, we have no idea what the next scene will hold. At one point, we even witness a main character die and then come "back to life" in the next scene.

While the narrative's forward and backward movement may seem random, it's actually extremely well placed. This film uses several Eastern ideas including the theme that violence begets more violence, and the only way to escape the circle of violence is to grant forgiveness. In the film, any character who seeks revenge or commits violence will continue to be caught up in the cycle of violence unless they forgive or are forgiven. In fact, if a character shows forgiveness, they are never seen in the film again (or only seen in a small capacity), as if escaping the film equates escaping the cycle of violence.

Jules and Vincent are two hitmen whose lives travel in drastically different directions. After coming close to death,

Jules has a major revelation and decides to forgive the two robbers at the diner instead of killing them. This forgiveness grants him his life, and he escapes the film unharmed. Jules, on the other hand, doesn't learn how to forgive, and he gets killed. Death, however, isn't strong enough to get him out of the cycle of violence, and he appears in another scene. Boxer Butch Coolidge wins a match when he was told by mobster Marcellus Wallace to lose. By all rights, in the violent world of *Pulp Fiction*, this should mean he's dead. While on the run, both he and Marcellus are kidnapped by a group of unsavory characters. While Butch has the opportunity to escape and leave Marcellus to die, he chooses instead to go back and save him. As a result, Marcellus forgives Butch, and they both are never seen in the film again. Forgiveness has granted Butch life where nothing else could have.

While the stories of these characters, fighting their way through violence and forgiveness, are told out of order, the Major Dramatic Curve is linear. The Place of Rest is the scene in the diner where we see violence for the first time. The Inciting Incident comes when Vincent and Jules arrive at the apartment where the suitcase thieves reside. Here, Jules invokes God (the ultimate forgiver) with his Biblical quote. From here on out, the battle rages with violence and all the possible outlets for violence to emerge. The Crisis Point is when Butch must decide between saving Marcellus or leaving him to die at the hands of the unsavory characters in the pawn shop. He makes the decision to save Marcellus, and then we see the violence getting "cleaned" (both metaphorically and literally) until we reach our Climax. We see Jules forgive the two diner robbers, Pumpkin and Honey Bunny, and the film ends. Forgiveness has destroyed violence, and the Major Dramatic Curve is complete.

While creating nonlinear stories requires a lot of extra work on behalf of the writer, there is a growing desire by consumers to see these kinds of narratives. Just make sure you justify the choice of nonlinear storytelling and keep that Major Dramatic Curve working in a linear progression to make the story work.

A Word About Television

Many believe we live in a Golden Age of television, and with such great narratives being created for the small screen, it's not a surprise to learn the impact this kind of storytelling has on other narrative forms. While we mentioned one form of television storytelling above with *Downton Abbey*, it's worth taking a moment to look at the two main kinds of storytelling narratives and how they relate to the Major Dramatic Curve and to other formats.

Television shows can exist as one of two kinds of structures: episodic or serials. In an episodic television show, the world and the characters of each episode are the same, but the story is not a direct continuation of the previous episodes. While there can be some development over the course of a season, the episodes are basically standalone tales that can be watched out of order. A great example is season one of *Supernatural*. Over the course of the first season, there is an overarching story of brothers Sam and Dean looking for their missing father, but the real attraction of the show is the Monster-Of-The-Week structure in which the brothers fought a new supernatural being each week.

When television first began, most television shows were episodic because it was common for viewers to miss an episode every now and then due to life's demands. With no recording equipment and no reruns, if a viewer missed an episode, there was no way they could see it after the original air date. As a result, television writers knew they had to tell stories limited to a single show. Early television shows like *The Lone Ranger* and *The Honeymooners* could be watched whenever the viewer could be home to watch the original airing, and missing an episode wouldn't affect the overall comprehension of plot.

With these kinds of shows, the plot is self-contained, and so the Major Dramatic Curve can exist as a fully developed unit unique to each episode. The crime fighter will take down the villain of the week. The doctor will heal the patient of the week. The CSI investigators will find the murderer of the week. These shows are self-contained and so the Curves are as well.

If the episodic has hints of a larger storyline (Sam and Dean looking for their father, Jim and Pam flirting across the desk, Moriarty getting closer to Sherlock, etc.), then a larger Curve can also exist that encompasses the entire season. The key thing to remember with episodics, however, is the episode specific Curves must be fully developed. This is true for other episodic narrative structures as well, including a collection of short stories (such as *The Joy Luck Club* by Amy Tan, *Orlando* by Virginia Wolf or *The House on Mango Street* by Sandra Cisneros), an episodic web-series (such as *Neil's Puppet Dreams*) or an episodic comic series.

After the invention of the VCR and later the TiVo/DVR systems, which allowed viewers to watch a show after the original air date, a new kind of television show became more popular: the serial. Taking its storytelling origins from serial comics and serial radio shows, a serial television show could tell a larger story over the course of multiple episodes or an entire season. While most of the first television serials were daytime soap operas, more "evening soaps" showed up after the VCR, including *Dallas* and *Knots Landing*. Today, serials make up the majority of our television lineup, and they aren't just soaps anymore: *Breaking Bad*, *Game of Thrones*, *Dexter*, *The Walking Dead*, *Silicon Valley*, *Orange is the New Black* and *Arrested Development* are only a few of the heavy hitters.

In these kinds of television shows, the key thing to remember about the Major Dramatic Curve is the main Curve must last the entire season. While there can be smaller goals in each episode, these episode-based goals are just tactics the protagonist uses to win his larger goal. In the HBO serial *Silicon Valley*, protagonist Richard wants to prove the validity of the file compression application he created. In the pilot episode, he leaves his day job to form his own company, and the main goal of season one is to get that company off the ground. While each episode has a minor goal (complete a successful business plan, secure the copyright for the name of his company, fixing code, conducting a successful presentation at a major award competition, etc.), all of these episode goals work to support the season-long goal of launching his company.

Other serial formats should also use this kind of narrative structure. Serial comics (like *Fables*), serial web series (such as *The Guild*) and serialized novels (Stephen King's *The Green Mile* or *The Dark Tower*, for example) also have a strong Major Dramatic Curve lasting the entire series. Uniting the individual episodes under one Major Dramatic Curve keeps the series feeling consistent and engaging for the reader/viewer.

Back in the world of television, as DVRs became more common and serials became more successful, a strange hybrid developed. Episodic television shows slowly morphed into something closer to a serial in later seasons. *House, Supernatural, Grimm* and *Once Upon A Time* are only a few examples. A similar thing happened in the later *Harry Potter, Divergent* and *The Hunger Games* book series as well. While the reasoning behind this morphing of structure is a direct result of how stories are sold in their respective industry (it's easier to sell a stand-alone narrative than one without a clear cut ending), it's important to study how the writers changed their underlying structure to reflect their new method of storytelling.

Let's look at *The Hunger Games*: the first book of the series has a clear cut Major Dramatic Curve, which we have revisited several times in this text. The first book is obviously part of a larger series (we are left wondering what will happen next when we reach the end of the novel), but it can also stand on its own. The next two books in the series, *Catching Fire* and *Mockingjay*, are written in a way that both mirrors the structure of the first book and contradicts it. All three books have a similar underlying structure: each one has some kind of a tour and then some kind of a game. In *The Hunger Games*, the tour is Katniss's choosing and journey to the Capitol where she explores that world before the Games. *Catching Fire* refers to the two sections as the Tour and the Games directly. In *Mockingjay*, Katniss's tour is her attempts at becoming the PR figure everyone wants her to be and then the Games is the journey into the Capitol where booby traps are set up in the streets. This similar underlying structure makes all three books feel a part of the same series so the reader doesn't feel like they were thrown into a completely new world.

Conversely, however, the way the Major Dramatic Curve operates in the texts changes. While *The Hunger Games* has its own, fully developed Major Dramatic Curve, the second and third books share a Curve. When President Snow shows up at her house, Katniss is incited to protect the people she loves, including Peeta. Her goal continues through the Tour and into the Games, where she does everything she can to make sure Peeta lives through the Games. Her goal is never reached, however, because the Games end suddenly. Peeta is taken to the Capitol, and Katniss has no choice but to wait before she can continue to fight for her goal. That goal isn't won until the very end of *Mockingjay*, after the deaths of many people including several major characters. While other goals surface along the way, Katniss has always been a selfish character, wanting to protect those she loves more than wanting to fix the world around her. As Suzanne Collins adapted from episodic to serial, she made sure to adapt the Major Dramatic Curve as well.

Create Your Own Exception

The Major Dramatic Curve is adaptable to any kind of narrative structure you are interested in using. It can be altered and manipulated in order to fit whatever form of framing you wish to put around your story, regardless of format. The only real rule you want to remember is that the Curve must exist in some way, shape or form in order to fully encompass Aristole's notions of beginning, middle and end and develop your complete Character Arc. As you move forward with your own writing adventure, ask yourself how you can creatively adapt the Curve to fit in with any narrative you wish to create.

Chapter 13
Your Inciting Incident

We have discussed how to build a character's personality and dialogue mechanics, and we have, at length, discussed how to formulate a fully developed Major Dramatic Curve. We have looked at how you can apply the Curve and how you can manipulate it to fit multiple protagonist and other non-traditional narrative structures. In short, I've done all I can to assist you in building a fully realized character arc.

You may still have lingering doubts about whether or not this structure will work for you. As we questioned in Part One: is it really possible for the artistic pursuit of writing to be compounded and regulated using such strict writing guidelines? Won't using the Major Dramatic Curve hinder my writing instead of enhancing it? Yes, it may have worked for thousands of stories in the past, but my story is so unique and so different, there's no way it will apply to me!

All I can say to these lingering doubts is this: you might be right. This Curve may not work for you and your story. You might be writing a film like Jim Jarmusch's *Broken Flowers* that ends at the crisis point. Or you might be writing a novel like Justin Cronin's *The Passage* that covers such a large expanse of time that it's hard to limit the story into one Arc. Or you may be writing a play such as *The Complete Works of William Shakespeare (Abridged)*, which is more about summarizing a number of other stories instead of just telling a single one.

However, most writers who are interested in any kind of commercial success know it's best to learn and practice the rules of good storytelling so you can break them later on. I've taught so many beginning writers in my workshops and classes who have wanted to be unique and different. They wanted to come up with something no one had ever seen before. While I applaud their ambition, I often find this desire to be different comes less from the need to be original and more for the desire to be a bit lazy. Instead of learning the "proper" way of writing, they want to just write from the heart and then collect their $1 million dollar advance.

Sadly, the industry doesn't work that way. Often, a novice writer needs to prove their ability to write a marketable work just to get their name on the shelves at their local bookstore. Once that first book is on the shelf, their agent can use that existing title to help promote the author's more experimental work. Similarly, most beginning screenwriters have to prove their ability to work within industry guidelines (formatting, genre conventions, etc.) before they are ever trusted with the creation of something more original. Theater tends to allow a bit more creativity from their beginning playwrights but considering that most playwrights usually see their first shows produced at smaller theaters – often community theaters – they usually find more success with great characters acting within a more traditional narrative structure.

In studying the craft of writing, I've come across many theories of writing. Some of them really didn't sit well with me. Blake Snyder's overly formulaic approach to screenwriting happened to be one of them. But I still gave it a try – mostly because it was a requirement in my formal education. As much as I hate to admit to the professor who forced me to use Snyder's Beat Sheet, using those guidelines increased my skills as a writer. I learned valuable lessons about pacing my story that I still use today, even though I have long since abandoned the notion of making sure specific events happen in my story on a certain page. Exposing my writing to new theories has always made me better, even if I didn't believe in the concepts themselves.

So even if you aren't entirely convinced that the Major Dramatic Curve structure is right for you, I give you this inciting incident: keep an open mind. Study the novels, films, plays and short stories you love most and see how the Curve operates in those narratives. Try applying the concepts discussed in this book to your own narratives and see if they give you clarity or inspiration on how you can make your stories stronger than they already are. The worst thing that can happen is you will grow as a writer. And that's a goal worth fighting for.

Appendixes

If there's a [story] you really want to read,
but it hasn't been written yet,
then you must write it.
— Toni Morrison

Appendix A
Studying Character

Throughout this textbook, we dived headfirst into a practical, step-by-step guide to creating a fully developed Character Arc. In order to help clarify the various concepts discussed, I referred to a number of narratives from varying formats. I have tried to be as well-rounded as possible in my narrative choices with the hope than anyone utilizing this text will have read, viewed or played at least some of the stories I mentioned. I will admit many of my choices look at films. This is not due to any prejudice against literature, plays, games or web series. This is simply because, in our modern culture, films have the widest reach, and I find many of these examples to be the most identifiable and relatable.

Below, you will find a complete list of the narratives I used throughout this text, accompanied by a one to two sentence description of that story. Feel free to use this list to give you a broad overview of the stories I examined. You may choose to view or read a few of these as a supplement to this textbook in order to cement the lessons covered.

21 Grams, Film, Screenplay by Guillermo Arriaga
A nonlinear story the focuses on three people affected by an accident that kills a young man and his daughter: the grieving widow/mother, the man who received a heart transplant from the deceased man and the Born Again ex-con responsible for the deaths.

The 40-Year Old Virgin, Film, Screenplay by Judd Apatow and Steve Carell
A 40 year old nerd befriends his colleagues at work. Once those colleagues discover he's a virgin, they will do anything to get him laid, including steering him away from a girl he actually cares about.

Atonement, Film and Book, Novel by Ian McEwen, Screenplay by Christopher Hampton
A young girl witnesses a horrible crime but makes an accusation against the wrong person. Years later, she realizes the horrible thing she has does and seeks to make amends in any way she can.

Avengers, Film, Screenplay by Joss Whedon, Based on characters from Marvel Comics
After a power-hungry alien steals a top secret weapon, a team of superheroes must find a way to overcome their differences in order to save Mankind.

Big, Film, Screenplay by Gary Ross and Anne Spielberg
A young boy wishes to be an adult, but when his wish comes true, he wants nothing more than to return to his life as a carefree youngster.

Bill & Ted's Excellent Adventure, Film, Screenplay by Chris Matheson and Ed Solomon
Two rock and roll wannabe teenagers travel through time in a magic phone booth in order to gather information that will allow them to pass their high school history class.

Breaking Bad, Television Series, Show Runner Vince Gilligan
A brilliant yet passive and prideful high school chemistry teaches gets diagnosed with lung cancer. In order to pay for his medical treatment and to take care of his family after his death, he begins cooking crystal meth. His meth is considered so pure and desirable, he quickly becomes a target of the more dangerous drug dealers in New Mexico.

Brokeback Mountain, Film, Screenplay by Larry McMurty and Diana Ossana, based on the short story by Annie Proulx
Two male cowboys fall in love in the homophobic landscape of 1963 Wyoming. Their relationship develops over the years, but their need to keep it a secret slowly destroys them both.

Chicago, Stage Musical, Book by Fred Ebb and Bob Fosse, Lyrics by Fred Ebb
An aspiring jazz singer goes to jail for shooting her lover. The press rockets her to the stardom she's always wanted, but if she isn't careful, she'll hang before she gets to enjoy it.

Chronicle, Film, Screenplay by Max Landis
After discovering a strange crystal, three high school boys develop super-hero powers, but one of the boys has been an underdog a bit too long. Instead of using his powers for good, he begins to turn into a new super villain.

Citizen Kane, Film, Screenplay by Herman J. Mankiewicz and Orson Welles
On his deathbed, a rich publishing tycoon utters a single word: "Rosebud." A news reporter then interviews a number of people who knew him, hoping to find the source behind the mystifying utterance.

Crash, Film, Screenplay by Paul Haggis
Several multicultural individuals living in Los Angeles intersect in ways that push their limits of racism and tolerance.

The Cuckoo's Calling, Novel, Written by Robert Galbraith
A down on his luck detective is given one last chance to get back on top when he is hired to investigate the apparent suicide of a famous celebrity.

Dark Places, Novel, Written by Gillian Flynn
The lone survival of her family's grisly homicide, a young woman must face the terrors of her past in order to prove her accused brother's innocence and find the real killer of her mother and sisters.

The Dark Tower, Novel Series, Written by Stephen King
A seven book series in which Roland Deschain, a gunslinger from a lost world of chivalry and courage, travels across a decaying Universe with three companions in an effort to save *The Dark Tower*, a structure that holds the multiple layers of the Universe together.

Dodgeball: A True Underdog Story, Film, Screenplay by Rawson Marshall Thurber
A group of losers try to save their beloved gym by competing in a professional dodgeball tournament. Unfortunately, their fierce rivals also sign up to compete in order to take them down.

Dominion 3: The Awakening, Game, created by Illwinter
Fantasy turn-based game in which the player creates a God. The player's God competes in a series of tactical battles with others an in attempt to rule over the entire land.

Downton Abbey, Television Series, Written by Julian Fellowes
An upstairs-downstairs drama that takes place in a British Manor in the days before the first World War. Due to the death of the estate's heir on the Titanic, the Lord of the Manor must find and train a new heir who will hopefully marry his eldest daughter.

Dr. Horrible's Sing-Along Blog, Web Series, Written by Joss Whedon, Zack Whedon, Maurissa Tancharoen and Jed Whedon
As aspiring super villain is given a chance to earn his place in the Evil League of Evil, but when his crush, a beautiful and altruistic girl, falls in love with his arch nemesis, a conceited jerk, getting into the League becomes deadly.

Edward Scissorhands, Film, Screenplay by Carolien Thompson
A half-completed yet extraordinarily kind Frankenstein of a man finds himself pulled into a suburban world that he can't quite understand or find a place to call home.

Epic Mickey, Game, created by Junction Point Studios
A Wii platform based game in which Mickey Mouse must save a dark version of the Magic Kingdom called the Cartoon Wasteland using paint and paint thinner. Along the way, he must overcome several nefarious characters including Oswald the Lucky Rabbit, Gremlin Gus and the Shadow Blot.

The Fifth Element, Film, Screenplay by Luc Besson and Robert Mark Kamen
After his dream girl falls into his cab, a former military special forces soldier turned cab driver does everything he can to win

her heart. Since she is a perfect being sent to save the Earth from a Great Evil, winning her over is going to be much harder than he thought.

Frozen, Animated Film, Screenplay by Jennifer Lee
Two young sisters are inseparable until the magical powers of one endangers the life of the other. The older sister hides her powers, but when they are unveiled on her 18th birthday, her sister must help her overcome her fears in order to save their beloved city and themselves.

Gone Girl, Novel, Written by Gillian Flynn
A man comes home to find his house destroyed and his wife missing. As the police try to discover what happened, all of the man's secrets go on display for a public audience excited to condemn him for a murder that may not have even occurred.

The Goonies, Film, Screenplay by Chris Columbus
After discovering a treasure map in his father's attic, a young boy and his friends set out to find a long lost buried treasure. When a local crime family finds out about the map, however, the group's life is suddenly in danger from a lot more than simple booby traps.

The Gunslinger, Novel and Graphic Novel, Written by Stephen King
The first book of *The Dark Tower* series, The Gunslinger follows Roland as he pursues the mysterious Man in Black. Along the way, Roland has to overcome many obstacles including a town determined to murder him, a vast desert landscape and his own growing feelings for a young boy from another world.

Hamlet, Play, Written by William Shakespeare
A young prince grieving from the loss of his father receives a message from a ghost accusing his uncle of murdering his father. The prince sets out to prove his uncle's guilt before finding the perfect way to avenge his father's death.

The *Harry Potter* Series, Novel Series, Written by JK Rowling
This seven book series follows Harry Potter, a young wizard whose parents were murdered by an evil wizard. On that same night, baby Harry mysteriously defeated the dark wizard, and he spends his school years learning more about how that happened and how he will defeat that same dark wizard in the future.

Harvester, Game, created by DigiFX Interactive
Point and click adventure in which a man wakes up with no memory. Over time, he learns the dark secrets of the small town in which he awakens.

Hot Fuzz, Film, Screenplay by Edgar Wright and Simon Pegg
After the best cop in London is reassigned to a small, picture-perfect village, he has to fight to convince the town that a string of strange deaths are murders and not accidents.

The Hunger Games, Film, Screenplay by Suzanne Collins, Billy Ray and Gary Ross
Film adaptation of the hit Young Adult book. First installment of the *The Hunger Games* series (see below).

The Hunger Games Series, Novel Series, Written by Suzanne Collins
This three book series follows Katniss Everdeen, a young woman who volunteers to compete in a fight to the death challenge in order to protect her younger sister. Her exploits in the Games turn her into a symbol of hope and revolution against a dystopian

Capitol government who watch the Games as a form of frivolous entertainment.

Interview With A Vampire, Novel, Written by Anne Rice
An young interviewer with a desire to become a vampire interviews a vampire who has struggled with this own identity since his turning in 18th century New Orleans.

Jerry Maguire, Film, Screenplay by Cameron Crowe
After writing a mission statement that gets him fired, an egotistical sports agent must fight to regain his self confidence and career while managing a growing relationship with his idealistic assistant.

The Joy Luck Club, Novel, Written by Amy Tan
Four sets of Chinese mothers and their first generation Chinese American daughters tell their stories of negotiating identity in a changing cultural landscape.

King Lear, Play, Written by William Shakespeare
A retiring King forces his daughters to tell him how much they love him in order to receive a portion of his Kingdom. The two daughters who spew their love for him wind up removing him from his position of power. Conversely, the one daughter who truly loves him but refused to play his game of pride fueled game, will do anything to save him from her treacherous sisters.

The Last of Us, Game, created by Naughty Dog
A PlayStation 3 platform based game in a future dystopian world where a fungus has infected mankind, turning them into flesh eating monsters. When a smuggler encounters a girl whose immune system may lead to finding a cure, he will do anything to save her.

The Legend of Zelda, Game, created by Nintendo
A young knight searches through the Kingdom of Hyrule, defeating monsters and collecting items, as he fights to save the Princess Zelda from the evil Ganondorf.

The Lego Movie, Film, Screenplay by Phil Lord and Christopher Miller
After falling down a hole and getting attached to a strange object, an ordinary construction worker learns of a prophecy naming him as "The Special," a hero who will destroy an evil Businessman and save the Lego empire.

The Lord of the Rings series, Novel and Film series, Novels written by J.R.R. Tolkien, Screenplays written by Peter Jackson, Fran Walsh and Philippa Boyens
Three book series in which a small creature known as a Hobbit must overcome monsters, men and his own inner demons in order to save the world.

Love Actually, Film, Screenplay by Richard Curtis
A series of vignettes about various couples (both romantic and not) living in modern day London and how their love develops, blossom, falls apart or ends happily.

Memento, Film, Screenplay by Christopher Nolan, based on the short story *Memento Mori* by Jonathan Nolan
A man who can't create new short-term memories must piece together the clues surrounding his wife's death.

Monty Python and the Holy Grail, Film, Written by Graham Chapman, John Cleese, Eric Idle, Terry Gilliam, Terry Jones and Michael Palin
King Arthur and his very silly Knights of the Round Table set off on a quest to find the Holy Grail. Along the way, they encounter

damsels in distress, creepy bridge-keepers, vicious bunnies, angry Gods, and some very rude Frenchmen.

Moulin Rouge!, Film, Screenplay by Baz Luhrman and Craig Pearce
A romantic writer moves to Paris to find love, but when he falls for a courtesan, his idealistic notions of what true love means are tested.

The Name of the Rose, Novel, Written by Umberto Eco
In a monastery in Northern Italy, a string of murders surfaces in which monks are found dead with black fingers and black tongues. A friar and his assistant seek out the clues that lead to uncovering the murderer and his dastardly modus operandi.

National Treasure, Film, Screenplay by Jim Kouf, Cormac Wibberley and Marianne Wibberley
An eccentric historian uses clues left on National Treasures, such as the Declaration of Independence, in order to find a long-lost buried treasure. He must hurry, however, since a violent thief also pursues the treasure, and he's willing to kill to get there first.

The Notebook, Novel and Film, Written by Nicholas Sparks, Screenplay by Jeremy Leven
An old man tells a story of young love to a woman with Alzheimer's. The young lovers must overcome class issues and their own miscommunications in order to find their happily ever after.

Paranormal Activity, Film, Screenplay by Oren Peli
A young couple set up a video camera in their bedroom to figure out the source of strange noises in the night. The camera footage reveals that the noises aren't caused by neighborhood kids, but by something demonic.

Pride and Prejudice, Novel, Written by Jane Austen
After an offensive first meeting, a carefree young woman and a socially lacking yet extremely wealthy gentleman fall in love despite the obstacles keeping them apart. These obstacles include her poor financial situation, his preconceived notions about people living in the country, her eccentric family and their pride.

The Princess Bride, Film, Screenplay by William Goldman
A grandfather reads a story of epic proportions to his sick grandfather. The story includes "fencing, fighting, torture, revenge, giants, monsters, chases, escapes, true loves, miracles" and a lot of humor.

The Proposal, Film, Screenplay by Pete Chiarelli
When threatened with deportation, a powerful executive editor at a publishing company blackmails her assistant into marrying her for a Green Card. The only trouble is that, as she gets to know him, she falls in love with him and his family along the way.

Pulp Fiction, Film, Screenplay by Quentin Tarantino
A nonlinear collection of four stories involving crime and violence in which the lives of two hit men, a boxer, a mob boss and his wife intersect amidst the transportation of a strange, glowing briefcase.

Romancing the Stone, Film, Screenplay by Diane Thomas
A romance novelists travels to Colombia in order to pay the ransom for her kidnapped sister. When she arrives, she gets lost in the jungles of South America and only a rough, American bird smuggler can help her find her way to her sister and to a long lost treasure.

Se7en, Film, Screenplay by Andrew Kevin Walker
Two detective, one at the end of his career, the other at the beginning of it, hunt down a serial killer who murders his victims in line with the seven deadly sins.

Silicon Valley, Television Series, Showrunner Mike Judge
A group of nerd friends band together to create a new software company, but their futures are threatened by their own business inexperience, an eccentric and unpredictable investor and a competing Google-like powerhouse business.

The Stand, Novel, Written by Stephen King
After a super virus wipes out the majority of mankind, the survivors gather together for the ultimate battle of good versus evil.

Supernatural: Season One, Television Series, Showrunner Eric Kripke
Two brothers seek for their missing father, all the while hunting supernatural monsters and a yellow-eyed demon responsible for murdering their mother.

The Sweet Hereafter, Film, Screenplay by Atom Egoyan, based on the novel by Russell Banks
A lawyer pieces together the events surrounding a school bus accident that resulted in the deaths of a small town's children.

There Will Be Blood, Film, Screenplay by Paul Thomas Anderson, loosely based on the novel *Oil!* By Upton Sinclair
A miner turns to oil in his pursuit for wealth. In his bid for power, he destroys everything in his way.

The Time Traveler's Wife, Novel, Written by Audrey Nifeneger
A man who time travels against his will forms a lifelong romance with his wife. Together, they face the same trials and tribulations faced by all couples, but they are forced to deal with them out of order.

The Town, Film, Screenplay by Peter Craig, Ben Affleck and Aaron Stockard, based on the novel *Prince of Thieves* by Chuck Hogan
A recovering drug addict begins a relationship with a woman he was forced to kidnap during a bank robbery gone wrong. He wants nothing more than to leave his crime life behind and run away with his new love, but a crime boss gives him a choice: participate in a dangerous heist that's sure to get him killed or see the love of his life murdered.

Toy Story, Animated Film, Screenplay by Joss Whedon, Andrew Stanton, Joel Cohen and Alex Sokolow
Jealous of a new toy introduced into his owner's bedroom, a cowboy doll pushes the new spaceman action figure out the window. He then must go on an adventure to rescue the spaceman from an evil next-door neighbor before their owner realizes they are gone.

Twilight, Novel and Film, Novel by Stephenie Meyer, Screenplay by Melissa Rosenberg
A teenager girl moves to Alaska where she meets and falls in love with a local vampire. As their relationship grows, so too does the danger around them, especially when a group of troublemaking vampires come to town.

Twilight: New Moon, Novel and Film, Novel by Stephenie Meyer, Screenplay by Melissa Rosenberg
After her beloved vampire leaves her, a young teenager will do

anything she can to get him back, even if it means starting a relationship with a local werewolf.

The Vanishing, Film, Original screenplay by Tim Krabbé (based on his novel), Updated screenplay by Todd Graff
After his wife goes missing, a man becomes obsessed with finding out what happened to his wife. When he meets her killer, he's given a choice: go through exactly what she went through or never know the truth

The West Wing, Television Series, Showrunner Aaron Sorkin
A day-in-the-life drama about lives of the staff working in the most famous office in the United States: The West Wing.

The Wizard of Oz, Film, Screenplay by Noel Langley, Florence Ryerson and Edgar Allan Woolf, based on the novel by L. Frank Baum
After a tornardo transports her home from rural Kansas to a magical land, a young girl must find a way home.

Wreck-It Ralph, Animated Film, Screenplay by Phil Johnston and Jennifer Lee
An arcade game villain fights to win a medal in order to prove to his game-mates that he's a hero. Unfortunately, when a sugared up race car gamers in another game steals his medal, he has to learn that there is more to being a hero than he first thought.

You've Got Mail, Film, Screenplay by Nora Ephron and Delia Ephron, based on the play *Parfumerie* by Miklós László
A small bookstore owner's shop is threatened when a corporately owned megabookstore moves in down the block. She fights for her company, never realizing she's been having an online romance with the company's owner.

Appendix B
What Was That Word Again?

Below is a quick guide to some of the vocabulary covered in this text.

Act One: the first thirty pages (or 1/4) of a motion picture screenplay in which the writer establishes the genre, main characters and main conflict of the story. This section is also known as the Setup or the Exposition.

Act Two: the middle sixty pages (or middle 1/2) of a motion picture screenplay, usually divided into two "quests." This is the meat and potatoes of the film, and as a result, it is the Conflict.

Act Three: the last 30 pages (or 1/4) of a motion picture screenplay in which the final big battle of the film occurs and all lose ends are resolved. This section is also known as the Resolution, even though it contains more than just the resolution of the story.

Active protagonist: A protagonist (see separate definition) who actively pursues a goal and takes an active role in his/ her fate.

Ally: a friend or acquaintance of the protagonist who aids the main character as he or she pursues the goal.

Antagonist: The character whose goal most directly conflicts with the goal of the protagonist. This term is not synonymous with villain, as the dramatic function of the antagonist has nothing to do with good versus evil.

Bonding Character: The most important secondary character whose actions result in the protagonist eventually winning the main goal.

Catch Phrase: A standalone phrase a character says that reflects the identity and personality of the character in that one statement. This is the kind of phrase which would appear on a T-shirt for marketing purposes.

Character: a combination of traits, morals, personality and attitudes that make up the individuals who exist within our stories and serve as a gateway of identification for readers and viewers

Character Arc: A pictorial representation of the process of development a character goes through over the course of a narrative.

Character mechanics: The technical tools a writer can use, especially in dialogue, to shape how a character appears to a reader or viewer

Climax: The moment where a protagonist wins or loses the main goal of the story. This should occur as close to the end of the narrative as possible.

Comic relief: A character whose primary dramatic function is to alleviate tension in a text. This character can be used merely for entertainment purposes or to reflect on broader themes or meanings within a text.

Crisis Point: A Point of No Return for the character that can vary based on the kind of story the writer wants to tell. The Crisis can be an emotional peak (high or low), a moral decision/crossroads or a source of new information.

Defining Action: The physical action a character performs when the reader/viewer is first introduced to the character. This first impression should help define the personality of the character for the reader/viewer.

Delivery: The method in which a character's meaning is conveyed to a listener.

Diction: Word choice. In regards to dialogue this can relate to the educational quality of the words, to the use of slang, or any cultural, economical or other influential factors.

Dramatic Function: The purpose a character has for existing in a text. This purpose refers to how the writer plans on using them as a narrative tool in the story and not to how the character interacts with the other characters or the plot.

Dues ex machina: "Machine of the Gods" is an expression from ancient Greek theater referring to a convenient ending that seems a little too coincidental to be believable or satisfying

Emotional Climax: The moment of cathartic release a reader or viewer experiences at the culmination of the B-story. This is usually not the same thing as a Major Dramatic Curve Climax (see above definition), but it can be the same in some narratives.

Expositional Character: A character whose dramatic function is to provide necessary information, explanation or backstory to the reader or viewer.

Falling Action: The short section of narrative after a climax when any remaining lose ends are tied up for the reader/viewer.

Freytag's Triangle: A pictorial representation of the dramatic functions of each of the five acts that made up the common theatrical productions of the 19th century.

Goal: Also called a Want, this is the tangible object a character fights to win or influence over the course of a narrative story.

Hero's Journey: Also known as a Monomyth, it is an underlying narrative structure based on mythology which was developed by Joseph Campbell

Imagery: The choice of visually description phrases a character or writer might use as part of his or her descriptions

Inciting Incident: The external event that launches the protagonist after his or her goal. This should occur approximately 1/12 of the way into any narrative.

Love Interest: A character whose dramatic function is to enter a romantic relationship with the protagonist

Major Dramatic Curve: A pictorial representation of the character arc that found its roots in the theater but have developed to have practical applications for any kind of narrative format including films, novels, short stories and games

Major Dramatic Question: A question that unifies the protagonist's goal and must be answered with a yes or no at the Climax. (i.e. Will Dorothy return home?)

Midpoint: In screenplay writing, an impactful event that divides Act Two into two separate quests.

Need: An emotional motivator for why the protagonist fights so hard to win his or her external/tangible goal/want.

New Place of Rest/Resolution: The protagonist's character as it stands after going through the adventure of the main narrative. This should be a reflection of where the character existed at the beginning of the tale.

Obstacle: Something that stands in the way of a character's attempt at winning a goal or in the way of a character succeeding at a tactic.

Personality: The combination of "Lego building block" traits that equate a unique and three-dimensional being

Plot Point One: In screenplay writing, the major event diving Act One from Act Two. This is usually where the stakes are raised, and the protagonist begins his or her most active attempts towards winning the goal.

Plot Point Two: In screenplay writing, the major event diving Act Two from Act Three. This is usually a Point of No Return, after which time the character can never go back to who they were at the beginning of the narrative. This is sometimes the same as the Crisis Point.

Plotters: Writers who plan out everything before they begin the main writing of a narrative.

Protagonist: The main character whose actions to win a goal most directly results in the main plot of the narrative.

Purgers: Writers who do not plan before they write and "discover" their characters and plot on the page as they go along.

Reactive Protagonist: A protagonist (see separate definition) who does not actively pursue a goal but instead reacts to the event happening around her and him. This character is usually much more passive and reflective.

Red Herring: A character whose dramatic function is through the reader or viewer of the trail of another character (i.e. a murderer).

Resting Period/Initial Place of Rest: Also known as the Ordinary World, this is the period of the Major Dramatic Curve in which the reader or viewer meets the character and the world of the narrative before the inciting incident.

Rising Action: This portion of the narrative makes up the majority of the Major Dramatic Curve. It is the uphill battle during which time the protagonist fights to win the goal. During this time, the protagonist will use a number of tactics as they encounter multiple obstacles that stand in their way. This is also the time where the character will learn the lessons needed or collect the items required to have a chance to win the final goal.

Save the Cat **Beat Sheet**: In screenplay writing, an underlying structure developed by Blake Snyder as a "paint-by-numbers" method of screenplay writing.

Scene goal: A tangible/visual objective for a character to fight for in an individual scene. Scene goals are usually tactics the characters uses towards winning their ultimate narrative goal.

Secret Item in the Closet: A physical object a character hides in their closet from their closest friends that reveals a secret which helps to define the character's core and create additional obstacles for the character. This Item in the closet is also useful in the creation of subtext.

Subtext: The hidden meaning existing under a line of dialogue, which is not directly stated by the character.

Syntax: the grammatical makeup of a sentence that reflects cultural and linguistic attitudes of the character speaking

Tactic: A strategy used by the protagonist to win his or her goal. When the tactic becomes the core of a scene, this tactic is usually also a scene goal (see definition above)

The Three Act Structure: In screenwriting, an updated model of Aristotle's narrative structure of beginning-middle-end. This structure, developed by Syd Field, divides a screenplay into four equal components (Act One, the beginning of Act Two, the end of Act Two, Act Three).

Villain: A character defined by his or her evil intentions. This character is not necessarily the story's antagonist, but the actions of this character will have an antagonistic impact on the protagonist's pursuit of winning the main goal.

Acknowledgments

A very special thanks to all the students I've taught, in my classrooms or attending my workshops, who helped me fine tune the information in this book over the years. Without their feedback, I would never have been able to grow and adapt these theories into the textbook you have before you. My students are my everything. I hope they all know how much they allow me to feel useful in this world.

Thank you also to Dr. Lee Beger and Michael Higgins, the two geniuses who first introduced me to the Major Dramatic Curve in my theater analysis and directing classes over twenty years ago.

Taking these concepts and creating this textbook couldn't have been possible without the assistance of several wonderful people. First of all, thank you to Matt Peters at Beating Windward Press - oh Editor my Editor - for believing in this book so completely and spending countless hours assisting me in getting it ready for publication. Next, thank you to the best writing group in the world: Allen Gorney, Julie Anne Wight and Heather Startup. I don't know where I would be if I didn't have the three of you to lean on and grow with each month. Thank you also to the others who have supported this project along the way, including Kristi Peters, Saritza Hernandez, Joshua Carlton, and those who have just generally supported me along the way, including Madeline Jarvis, Bud Jarvis (RIP Daddy), Stacy, Carlos and the Mejia clan, Lynda and Mike Mitchem, Tracy and Jeremy Reinhard, Jessica Straw, Tami Polansky, and my fellow writers at 5writers.com: Brad Windhauser, Darlene Cah, Linda Price, Ron Hayes and Emilia Fuentes Grant.

Finally, thanks to my beloved husband Phil, my wonderful partner in life that possesses the sense to get our fur-baby Tucker to leave me alone when I'm trying to write. Phil - nothing warms my heart more than knowing you fully and completely support me as a writer. I love you. I'm so grateful *Murder by Death* brought us together.

About the Author

Jennie Jarvis worked in the film and television industry in several major cities around the world including Los Angeles, New York, London and San Francisco. While working in Beverly Hills, she served as a script analyst, producing coverage for producers, investors, actors and writers. She worked as a freelance script consultant for over fifteen years working with clients around the world, and wrote and directed a number of short narrative and documentary films. Major credits include *The Matrix: Reloaded*, *The Matrix: Revolutions*, *Accepted*, *American Idol* and more.

Since moving to Florida, Jennie successfully built and coordinated screenwriting competitions as well as served as a judge for literary, film and theater competitions. She earned an MA in English from the University of North Florida and an MFA in Creative Writing from Queens University of Charlotte. She teaches screenwriting at Full Sail University in Winter Park, Florida.

As a published literary writer, she is a co-owner of the blog 5writers.com and has an active social media platform. She won awards for her screenplays, essays, poetry and short fiction, and has appeared in *Writer's Digest Magazine* and *The Florida Writer*. She is the Faculty Chairperson for the Florida Writers Association Annual Conference and regularly conducts networking and writing workshops.

Jennie can be contacted via:
 www.jenniejarvis.com
 www.facebook.com/JarvisWrites
 twitter.com/JarvisWrites
 tumblr.jarviswrites.com